# GUIDE TO
# BECOMING
# RICH

*WITHOUT* CUTTING UP
YOUR CREDIT CARDS

# Other Bestselling Books by
# Robert T. Kiyosaki & Sharon L. Lechter

## Rich Dad Poor Dad
What the Rich Teach Their Kids About Money That the Poor and Middle Class Do Not

## Rich Dad's CASHFLOW Quadrant
Rich Dad's Guide to Financial Freedom

## Rich Dad's Guide to Investing
What the Rich Invest In That the Poor and Middle Class Do Not

## Rich Dad's Rich Kid Smart Kid
Give Your Child a Financial Head Start

## Rich Dad's Retire Young Retire Rich
How to Get Rich Quickly and Stay Rich Forever

## Rich Dad's Prophecy
Why the Biggest Stock Market Crash in History Is Still Coming...
And How You Can Prepare Yourself and Profit from It!

## Rich Dad's Success Stories
Real Life Success Stories from Real Life People
Who Followed the Rich Dad Lesson

## Rich Dad's Guide to Becoming Rich
## Without Cutting Up Your Credit Cards
Turn "Bad Debt" into "Good Debt"

# GUIDE TO BECOMING RICH

## *WITHOUT* CUTTING UP YOUR CREDIT CARDS

By Robert T. Kiyosaki with Sharon L. Lechter, C.P.A.
The Authors of *Rich Dad Poor Dad*

WARNER
BUSINESS
BOOKS™

NEW YORK    BOSTON

Published by Warner Books in association with CASHFLOW Technologies, Inc., and BI Capital, Inc.

CASHFLOW and Rich Dad are registered trademarks of CASHFLOW Technologies, Inc. Rich Dad's Advisors is a trademark of CASHFLOW Technologies, Inc.

 are trademarks of CASHFLOW Technologies, Inc.

Warner Business Books
Warner Books

Time Warner Book Group
1271 Avenue of the Americas, New York, NY 10020
Visit our Web sites at www.twbookmark.com and www.richdad.com.

The Warner Business Books logo is a trademark of Warner Books.

Printed in the United States of America

First Printing: December 2003
10  9  8  7  6  5  4

Library of Congress Cataloging-in-Publication Data

Kiyosaki, Robert T.
    Rich dad's guide to becoming rich without cutting up your credit cards / Robert T. Kiyosaki and Sharon L. Lechter.
        p.    cm.
    ISBN 0-446-69752-4
    1. Finance, Personal.    2. Consumer credit.    3. Debt.    4. Financial security.    I. Lechter, Sharon L.    II. Title.
    HG179 .K644    2003
    332.024'01—dc22                                                        2003018909

# Contents

# *Introduction*

The question really is:

WHO *DOESN'T* WANT TO BE A MILLIONAIRE?

Recently, the most popular show on American television was *Who Wants to Be a Millionaire*. It was an overnight success not only here, but worldwide, with different on-air hosts in different countries. All you had to do, of course, was answer a series of trivia questions, and with each correct response, you earned more cash—right up to the jackpot of one million dollars!

The question "Who wants to be a millionaire?" became a popular catch phrase everywhere. Let's face it—with so much fixation on shows about money, getting rich, stock market millionaires, and huge lottery payouts, it leads us to the question, "Who *doesn't* want to be a millionaire?"

And yes, it is possible to win a million dollars on a game show. It is also possible to get millions of dollars by winning the lottery. And it is possible to become a millionaire by investing in an IPO (initial public offering). Then you could retire rich for the rest of your life. In fact, there are more ways to become rich today than in any other time in our history. Maybe that is why there is such an international frenzy over the idea of *getting rich*—and the quicker the better.

I was recently on television talking about my book *Rich Dad Poor Dad*. The interviewer asked, "Come on, why don't you tell us the truth? Didn't you write your book simply to take advantage of this get-rich-quick craze that is sweeping the nation?"

Her question really surprised me and I was almost at a loss for words. Finally, after regaining my thoughts, I replied, "You know, I never saw it that way. I can see why you would think I would write a book just for that reason. I wish I could say I was that smart. Smart enough to time my book for just this moment in history, but I am afraid I am not that smart. I wrote this book because I wanted to tell the story of the money lessons I learned from my two dads."

When I wrote the book in 1997, every bookstore and book distributor we approached turned it down. For that matter, in 1997, *Who Wants to Be a Millionaire* was not yet a TV show. I paused and said, "In fact, my book actually represents the exact opposite message of these game shows, stock market millionaires, and lotteries." Again I paused, thinking for a moment, and then continued, "There is indeed a frenzy today about getting rich quick and while my book is about getting rich, it is *not* about getting rich quick."

The commentator nodded and grinned a skeptical grin. "So if you are not part of this get-rich-quick mania, then what are you? Get rich slowly?"

I could feel her sarcasm and it challenged me. In front of millions of viewers I had to try to keep my cool. So I forced a chuckle in response to her barbed comment and said, "No, my book is not about getting rich quickly or getting rich slowly." I then smiled and waited for her to ask me the next question. The silence was deadly but I held my ground as calmly as possible, waiting for her to make the next move.

She smiled and asked, "So what is your book about?"

I grinned and replied, "It is about the price of getting rich."

"The price?" she replied. "What do you mean by the price?"

As she asked the question, the producer signaled to her that we were out of time. She then urged me to hurry with my answer and I ended the interview by saying, "Most everyone wants to get rich. But the problem is, only a few people are willing to pay the price."

The TV interview was over. The host thanked me and they cut to the final commercial. The problem was, I never answered what I think the price of becoming a millionaire is. This book answers the question that was not answered on that television interview.

## *Who Pays the Price?*

The U.S. Department of Health, Education, and Welfare tracked people from age twenty to sixty-five. Their findings were as follows:

By age sixty-five, per 100 people:

| | |
|---|---|
| 1 | was wealthy |
| 4 | were well off |
| 5 | were still working because they had to |
| 54 | were living on family or government support |
| 36 | were dead |

In addition, more than 35 percent of that wealthy 1 percent inherited their wealth, as did a large percentage of the 4 percent that were well off. As an additional note, *Forbes* magazine defines the rich as individuals with an income of over $1 million a year.

With the economic boom of the last ten years of the twentieth century, there was an increase in the number of wealthy and well off. Yet, the question remains, what did the top 5 percent who are rich do that the others did not? What was the difference in price the 5 percent paid that the others did not pay?

## Does a Big House Mean You're Rich?

When I was young, my rich dad drove me past a classmate's house, located in a very rich neighborhood. I asked rich dad if my classmate's dad was rich. Rich dad chuckled and responded, "A high-income job, a big house, nice cars, and lavish vacations do not mean you're rich. In fact it could mean exactly the opposite. A lavish lifestyle does not mean you're smart or well educated. It could mean exactly the opposite."

Most of us are wise enough to understand what rich dad meant by that statement. Yet, I think one of the reasons so many people faithfully play the lottery is because they too would like to have a nice big house, expensive cars, and all the other toys that money can buy. While it is possible to gain millions by winning the lottery, in reality, the chances are extremely slim. Just as a big house does not necessarily mean you're rich, sitting around watching a game show, or betting on your lucky numbers, is not the price that most of the top 1 percent paid to become rich.

## What Is the Price of Becoming a Millionaire?

There are many different ways to become rich. Winning the lottery or winning on a game show are just two examples. You can also become rich by being cheap, becoming a crook, or even marrying a millionaire. Many people actively look for millionaires to marry. Of course, be forewarned: With any method of attaining great wealth, there is a price, and the price is not always measured in money.

The *price* for sitting around and watching game shows and betting on the lottery is that *the vast majority of the viewers will never become rich . . . and that is a very steep price to pay.* There are better ways to become rich, with much better odds, but most people are not willing to pay the price. In fact, there are some ways of becoming rich in which the odds are in the person's favor, almost guaranteeing that a person will become rich, but again the problem is that most people are not willing to pay the price. And that is why, according to the Department of Health, Education, and Welfare, only 1 out of 100 people actually become rich, in the richest country in the world. They want to be millionaires, but they are not willing to pay the price.

So what did my rich dad mean by the price? Using a different example to explain the concept of *price* best explains this idea. What if I said, "I wish I had a body like Arnold Schwarzenegger." Well, the first thing most of you would say to me is, "Put on your running shoes, do five miles a day, go to the gym for three hours a day, and stop stuffing your face with pizza." To which I would say, "Is there another way to have a body like Arnold's?" That is what I mean by the price. Millions of people would like to have a great body but few people are willing to pay the price. And that is why ads that promise, "You will lose weight and still be able to eat all you want. Just take this little magic pill," or, "You can look like this gorgeous model without exercise or dieting," make so much money. Regardless if it's money, a sexy body, great relationships, happiness, or whatever we as humans have a desire for, Madison Avenue will come up with an ad campaign that promises the quick and easy way to get what you want. However, most of the products the ads promote do not work, not because of the products, but because the people who buy them are not willing to do the work (or pay the price).

I often refer to the $385 real estate investment course I purchased from a television infomercial many years ago. I remember sitting at home surfing the channels when I came across this infomercial. The ad encouraged me to come to a free evening seminar at the Hilton Hawaiian Village, a hotel on the beach at Waikiki right next to the condominium where I lived. I called to make my reservation for the free seminar; attended the free seminar; and then signed up for the $385 weekend seminar. I was still in the Marine Corps at that time, so I invited a fellow Marine pilot to go with me to the weekend seminar. He hated the seminar, called it a complete rip-off, a waste of time, and asked for his money back. Back at the squadron he said to me, "I knew it was going to be a rip-off. I should never have listened to you."

My experience was completely different. I left the seminar, took the books and tapes, read and listened to them, and have made millions of dollars from the information I learned from that seminar. As a friend of mine said to me a number of years later, "The problem with your friend was that he was too smart and did not get anything from the course. You were stupid enough to believe the instructor and went out and did what he taught you."

Today, I continue to recommend that people sign up for seminars to learn the basics of buying real estate, starting a business, investing in stocks, or whatever. I often hear back from the audience, "But what if the course is no good. What if I get ripped off? What if I don't learn anything? Besides, I don't want to fix toilets or have midnight phone calls from tenants." When I hear such comments, I usually reply, "Then it is best you do not attend the seminar. The seminar will definitely be a rip-off."

In my experience, many people are looking for the answers that will make their lives better in some way. The problem is, when they find the answer they don't like it . . . just as I don't like the answer, "Stop stuffing your face with pizza and start pumping iron for three hours day." In other words, until I like the answer I'm getting, I don't have a prayer of developing a body like Arnold Schwarzenegger. The reason most people will never become rich is simply because they don't like the answers they are getting. And in my opinion, it has little to do with the answer; it is the price that is attached to the answer that the person really does not like. As rich dad said, "Most people want to get rich. They just don't want to pay the price."

Now, in this book, I discuss the price of becoming rich without being cheap, immoral, crooked, or needing to marry a rich person. You will learn how to be rich and still enjoy a very rich lifestyle. But there is a price . . . and as my rich dad often said to me, "The price of something is not always measured in money." I share the answers and the price I paid. If you don't like my answers or my rich dad's answers, remember there is more than one way to become rich . . . there will always be a new lottery and game show that asks the question, "Who Wants to Be a Millionaire?"

*Chapter 1*

# What Is the Price of Being Cheap?

"The price of something is not always measured in money."
— RICH DAD

There are many books that popularize the idea of frugality and living below your means. Many so-called money experts write, speak, or broadcast on radio and TV the virtues of cutting up your credit cards, saving money, putting the maximum amount into your retirement plan, driving a used car, living in a smaller house, clipping coupons, shopping at sales, eating at home, passing used clothes from older kids down to the younger kids, taking cheaper vacations, and other such tips.

While these are excellent ideas for most people, and while there is a time and place for frugality, most people do not like these ideas. The truth for most people is that they love to enjoy the finer things of life that money can buy. For most people, a big home, a new car, fun toys, and expensive vacations are much more fun and desirable than putting money away in a bank. Most of us tend to agree with the wise sages professing frugality and economic abstinence. Yet, deep down, many of us would rather have a platinum credit card without a spending limit . . . that is paid for by your rich uncle who has more money than all the Arab oil sheiks, private Swiss banks, and Bill Gates combined.

While most of us enjoy the wonderful things money can buy, we realize that it is the unbridled desire for the fun, fine, and fancy things of life that gets many of us in financial trouble. And it is the financial trouble that these desires spawn that causes the money gurus to say, "Cut up your credit cards. Live below your means. Buy a used car."

On the other hand, my rich dad *never* said to me, "Cut up your credit cards." He *never* said, "Live below your means." Why would he advise me to do things he personally did not believe in? When it came to the idea of frugality, he did say, "You can become rich by being cheap. But the problem is, even though you're rich, you're still cheap." He would further say, "It makes no sense to me to live cheap and die rich. Why would anyone want to live cheap, die rich, and then have the kids spend your life's savings after the funeral?" Rich dad noticed that people who scrimped and saved all their lives often had children who acted like starving hyenas once the parents were gone. Instead of enjoying their parents' inheritance, they often fought over the money and spent it all soon after they got their hands on what they called their "fair share."

Instead of telling me to live cheaply, rich dad often said, "If you want something, find out the price, then pay the price." He also went on to say, "But always remember, everything has a price. And the price for becoming rich by being cheap is that you're still cheap."

## *The Different Ways You Can Become Rich*

Rich dad went on to explain, "You can become rich by marrying someone for his or her money. But we all know the price of that. I had a classmate in New York who often said, 'It is just as easy to marry a rich girl as a poor girl.' When he graduated, he married into a very rich family just as he said he would. I personally think he was a slimeball, but that was his way of becoming rich."

You can become rich by becoming a crook, and we all know the price of that choice. When I was a kid, I thought a crook wore a mask and robbed banks. Today, I realize that there are many crooks that wear blue suits, white shirts, red ties, and who are often respected members of their community.

There are others who become rich by betting at the casino or racetrack, on the lottery, or blindly throwing their money into the stock market. We know the price of that. During the dot-com mania, I knew many people who were ready to write a check if all you said was, "I'm starting an Internet company."

You can become rich by being a bully and we all know what happens to a bully. Eventually, an even bigger bully comes along, or the bully finds that the only people willing to do business with him or her are people who enjoy being pushed around.

And as described earlier, you can become rich by being cheap and we all know that the world tends to despise rich people who are cheap . . . people like Scrooge in Charles Dickens's classic *A Christmas Carol*. Most of us have met people who always want a larger discount, complain about the bill, or even worse, refuse to pay the bill for one frivolous reason or another. A friend who owns a dress shop often complains about the type of customer who buys a dress, wears it to a party, and then returns it a few days later, asking for her money back. And of course, there are those who drive old cars, wear clothes too long, buy cheap shoes, and look poor and yet have millions of dollars in the bank. While these individuals can become rich with such cheapness, there is a price far beyond money for such behavior. I personally struggle with being too cheap at times, and yet I notice that people tend to smile more or like me more when I am generous. For example, when I tip a little extra for good service, it comes back to me in other ways. In other words, people tend to like generous people more than cheap people.

## Can Everyone Be Rich?

Rich dad and I talked further about the price of being rich. He told me, "The price is different for different people."

Rich dad also said, "The only people who think life should be easy are lazy people."

Not being satisfied, I pressed on with my questioning. What did he mean by the price is different for different people. His reply was, "I would like to think that we all come into this world with unique gifts and talents . . . gifts and talents such as singing, painting, athletics, writing, parenting, preaching, teaching, and so on. But just because God gave us these talents, it is still up to each of us to develop those talents . . . and developing those talents is often the price. The world is filled with smart, talented, and gifted people who are not what we would call successful financially, professionally, or in their personal relationships. While each of us has gifts, each of us has personal challenges to overcome. No one is perfect. Each of us has gifts and challenges, strengths and weaknesses. That is why I say, the price is different for different people because each of us has different challenges. The only people who think life should be easy are lazy people."

I do not know if rich dad's statement about lazy people is true or not. I do know that his statement has been useful for me, whenever I found myself complaining about things not being easy, or things not going my way. When I find myself saying, "I wish things were easier," I know I am getting lazy. So whenever I find myself wishing things would be easier, I take a break, check my attitude, and ask myself about the long-term price of having that attitude. It's not that I don't look for an easier way to do things. I am simply aware of when I tend to be lazy, cheap, or when I act like a spoiled brat, and then I ask myself what the price might be for that behavior.

## Money Is the Reward for Paying the Price

Rich dad would also say, "Ask anyone who is rich, famous, or successful, and I am sure they will tell you that they had and have personal challenges and demons to face every day along the way. Son, there is no free lunch. My challenge was that I had no education and no money when I started out. I also had a family to feed when my father died. I was thirteen years old when I was given that challenge . . . and there were even greater challenges to come. Yet, I managed to pay the price, and in the end, I achieved great wealth. In hindsight, money was my reward for paying the price."

## The Price of Security

Over the years, rich dad made sure his son, Mike, and I were always aware of the price of something. When my dad, the man I call my poor dad, advised me to "Find a safe secure job," rich dad's reply was, "Remember, there is a price for security." When I asked him what the price was, he answered, "For most people, the price of security is personal freedom. And without freedom, many people spend their lives working for money, rather than living out their dreams. To me, to live life without achieving my dreams is much too high a price to pay for security." He also made his usual comment on taxes, by saying, "People who seek security over freedom pay more in taxes.

That is why people who have safe, secure jobs pay more in taxes than people who own the business that provides the jobs."

I spent a few days thinking about that comment, letting the magnitude of the idea sink in. The next time I saw rich dad, I asked him, "Do I have to choose between security or freedom? In other words, does that mean I can have one but not the other?"

Rich dad laughed after he realized how much thought I had given to his remark. "No," he replied, still chuckling. "You don't have to have one *or* the other. You can have both."

"You mean I can have both security and freedom?" I asked.

"Sure," he said. "I have both."

"So why did you say that for most people, the price of security is personal freedom?" I asked. "How can you have both when you say most people can have only one. What's the difference?"

"The price," said rich dad. "I've always said to you that everything has a price. Most people are willing to pay the price for security, but they are not willing to pay the price for freedom. That is why most people have only one of the two. They only have one or the other."

"And why do you have both security and freedom?" Mike asked. He had just entered the room and had heard only part of the conversation.

"Because I paid twice the price," said rich dad. "I was willing to pay the price for both security and freedom. It's no different than having two cars. Let's say I need a truck but I also want a sports car. If I want both, I pay twice the price. Most people go through life paying for one or the other, but not both."

"We pay *a* price even if we don't pay *the* price," rich dad continued.

"So there is a price for security and there is a price for freedom. And you paid the price for both." I repeated what rich dad had just said, so I could let the idea sink into my head.

Rich dad nodded his head. "Yes, but let me add one more point of clarity about my being willing to pay the price to have both. You see we all pay a price anyway. We pay a price even if we don't pay the price."

"What?" I replied, frowning and shaking my head. Rich dad now seemed to be speaking in circles.

"Let me explain," said rich dad, gesturing with his hands that we should calm down. "Do you remember when I helped the two of you with your science homework a few weeks ago? You were studying Newton's laws?"

Mike and I nodded.

"Do you remember the law of *for every action there is an equal and opposite reaction?*"

Again we nodded. "That is how a jet flies through the air," said Mike. "The engine propels hot air backward and the jet moves forward."

"That's right," said rich dad. "Since Newton's laws are universal laws, they apply to everything, not only jet engines." Rich dad looked at the two of us to see if we were following what he had just said. "Everything." He again repeated just to make sure we understood.

"Okay, everything," said Mike, a little frustrated at the repetition.

Suspecting that we were not really getting his point about *everything*, rich dad continued, "By everything I mean everything," he continued on. "Do you recall my lessons about financial statements? Do you remember my explaining that for there to be an *expense*, there must be *income* somewhere else?"

Now I was beginning to understand what he meant by "everything." Newton's universal laws also applied to financial statements. "So for every asset, there has to be a liability." I added just to let him know that I was beginning to follow his thinking: "A universal law applies to everything."

"And for something to be *up*, something else must be *down*," added Mike. "And for something to be *old*, something else has to be *new*. As Einstein said, 'It's all relative.'"

"Correct," rich dad said with a smile.

"So how does this apply to security and freedom and your being willing to pay twice the price?" asked Mike.

"Good question," said rich dad. "It's important because if you don't pay twice the price, you never get what you want anyway. In other words, if you don't pay twice the price, you do not get what you paid for in the first place."

"What?" I replied. "If you don't pay twice you don't get what you paid for?"

Rich dad nodded his head and began to explain. "People who pay the price only for security may never really feel secure . . . like in job security," he stated boldly. "A person may have a false sense of security, but they never really feel secure."

"So even though my dad has what he thinks is a safe, secure job, deep down he never really feels secure?" I asked.

"That's correct," said rich dad. "Because he is paying only for the action but not his internal reaction. The harder he works for security, or pays the price for security, the more his insecurity grows inside him."

"Does it have to be insecurity as the reaction?" Mike asked.

"Good question," rich dad commented. "No, it could be something else that is reacting. A person could have so much security that the reaction is boredom and then restlessness. They want to move on, but they don't move on because then they would give up their security. So that is why I say each of us has different challenges, each of us is unique. We're unique because we don't react to things in the same ways that others do."

"Like some people see a snake and panic, and others see a snake and get happy," I added.

"That's correct. We are all different because we are all wired differently," rich dad added.

"So what is the point of all this mental gymnastics?" I asked.

"The gymnastics are to make you think," said rich dad. "I always want you to remember that everything has a price . . . and that the price is often *twice* as much as it seems. If you pay for only one side of Newton's law, you may think you have paid the price but you may not get what you want."

"Can you give us some examples?" I asked.

"I can give you general ones because, as I said, each of us is unique," said rich dad. "But as a general rule, always remember there are two sides to each situation.

"For instance, the best employer has usually started his or her career as an employee. He or she uses that prior experience as an employee to develop a management style that empowers the employees he or she manages."

"So a good employer will be honest and treat his or her employees how he or she would like to be treated?" I asked.

"Exactly." Rich dad nodded. "Now let's look at an extreme example. What do you think it takes to be a good detective?"

"To be a good detective?" Mike and I repeated in tandem, thinking that rich dad was now driving down the wrong side of the road.

"Yes, a good detective," rich dad continued. "To be a good detective, a detective must first be honest, moral, and of the highest integrity. Is that correct?"

"I would hope so," said Mike.

"But to be good, a detective must also think exactly like a crook, or someone who is immoral, unlawful, and unethical," said rich dad. "Always remember Newton's law. You cannot be a good detective without *also* being able to think like a good crook."

Mike and I were now nodding. We were finally beginning to understand where rich dad was going with this whole lesson. "So that is why a person who tries to become rich by being cheap still winds up, in many ways, as poor as someone who has no money?"

Rich dad continued, "And why someone who seeks *only* security never really feels secure. Or someone who seeks low-risk investments never feels investing is safe, and someone who is always right eventually winds up wrong. They pay the price for one side of the equation but fail to pay the full price. They violate a universal law."

Mike chimed in, "That is why it takes two people to have a fight. And to be a good detective you have to also be a good crook. To lower risk, you have to take risks. To be rich you have to know what it is like to be poor. To know what a good investment is, you have to also know what a bad one is."

"And that is why most people say investing is risky," I added. "Most people think that to invest in a safe investment you must also lower your return on the investment. That is why so many people put money in a savings account. They put it in for security and are willing to take less interest for that safety. But the fact is, their money is being eaten away by inflation and the interest on their money is taxed at a high rate. So their 'safe as money in the bank' idea is not such a safe idea."

Rich dad concurred. "Having money in the bank is better than not having money in the bank . . . but you are correct by saying that it's not as safe as they may like to think it is. There is a price for that illusion of safety."

Mike then turned to his dad and said, "You've always said that it's possible to have both low-risk investments and very high returns."

"Yes," replied rich dad. "It is relatively easy to get a 20 percent to 50 percent return without paying a lot in taxes or using much of your own money, if you know what you are doing—and still have security."

"So what you're telling us now," Mike said, "is that the price you paid was higher than what the average investor is willing to pay."

Rich dad nodded. "Always remember that everything has a price, and that price is not always measured in money."

## *The Price of Being Cheap*

When I hear money gurus saying, "Cut up your credit cards, buy a used car, live below your means," I know they mean well. And for most people, their advice is good advice. But as my rich dad said, "Everything has a price." And the price for becoming rich by being cheap is that you still wind up being cheap. And living life as a rich but cheap person is, in my opinion, a very expensive price to pay.

Rich dad also said, "The problem is not the credit cards—it is the lack of financial literacy of the person holding the credit card that is the problem. Getting financially literate is part of the price you need to pay to become rich."

And that is why so many people do not like the idea of cutting up their credit cards and living below their means. I think most people, given the choice, would rather enjoy this life as *rich people* who enjoyed *rich lives* . . . and they can, if they are willing to pay the price.

## Chapter 2

# What Is the Price of a Mistake?

"My banker has never asked me for my report card."

— RICH DAD

At the age of fifteen, I failed the subject of English. I failed English because I could not write, or I should say, my English teacher did not like what I wrote about. And, my spelling was horrible. That meant I would have to repeat my sophomore year. The emotional pain and embarrassment came from many fronts. First of all, my dad was the Superintendent of Education for the island of Hawaii and in charge of over forty schools. There was snickering and laughter throughout the halls of education as the word spread from school to school that the boss's son was an academic failure. Second, failing meant I was going to join my younger sister's class. In other words, she was moving forward and I was moving backward. And third, it meant I would not receive my athletic letter for playing varsity football, the sport for which I had played my heart out. The day I received my report card and saw the F for English, I went behind the building that housed the chemistry lab to be alone. I sat down on the cold concrete slab, pulled my knees up to my chest, pushed my back up against the wooden building, and began to cry. I had been expecting this F for a few months, but seeing it on paper brought out all the emotions suddenly and uncontrollably. I sat alone behind the lab building for over an hour.

The good news was that my best friend, Mike, rich dad's son, had also received an F. It wasn't good that he failed too, but it was good that I at least had some company to go along with my misery. I waved to him as he headed across the campus to catch his ride home, but all he did was shake his head and kept on walking.

That evening, after my siblings had gone to bed, I told my mom and dad that I had failed English and would have to repeat my sophomore year of high school. At that time, the educational system had a policy requiring a student failing either English or Social Studies to repeat the entire year. My dad, who ran the educational system of the island, was quite familiar with the policy. While they had expected this news, the confirmation of my failure was still a difficult reality. My dad sat quietly and nodded. His face was expressionless. My mom, on the other hand, was having much more difficulty. I could see the emotions on her face . . . emotions that went from sadness to anger. Turning to my dad she said, "What's going to happen now? Will he be held back?" All my dad would say in reply was, "That's the policy. But before I make any decision, I'll look into the matter."

For the next few days, my dad, the man I refer to as my poor dad, did look into the matter. My dad discovered that out of my class of thirty-two, the teacher had failed fifteen of us. The teacher had given Ds to eight students. One student had an A, four had Bs, and the rest Cs. With such a high failure rate, my dad stepped in. He did not step in as my father, but as the Superintendent of Education. His first step was to order the principal of the school to open a formal investigation. The investigation began with interviews of the students in the class. The investigation ended with the teacher being transferred to another school and a special summer school offered to students who wanted an opportunity to improve their grades. I spent three weeks that summer working my way up to a D in English and was able to move on to the eleventh grade with the rest of my class.

My dad found that there were rights and wrongs with both the students and the teacher. What disturbed my dad was that most of those who failed were the top students in the sophomore class. Most of us were on track to go on to college. So rather than take a side, he came home and said to me, "Take this academic failure as a very important lesson in your life. You can learn a lot or you can learn a little from this incident. You can be angry, blame the teacher, and hold a grudge. Or you can look at your own behavior and learn more about yourself and grow from the experience. I don't think the teacher should have awarded so many failing marks. But I do think you and your friends need to become better students. I hope both the students and the teacher grow from this experience."

I must admit I did hold a grudge, I still don't like the teacher, and I hated going to school after that. I never liked being told to study subjects I was not interested in or knew I would never use once school was over. Although the emotional scars were deep, I did buckle down a little more, my attitude changed, my study habits improved, and I graduated from high school on schedule. I was also one of two students awarded a congressional appointment to the U.S. Merchant Marine Academy, from which I graduated in 1969, with a Bachelor of Science degree.

At the Academy I overcame my fear of writing and actually learned to enjoy it, although I am still a poor writer technically. I thank Dr. A. A. Norton, who was my English teacher for two years at the Academy, for helping me overcome my lack of self-confidence, my past fears and my grudges. If not for Dr. Norton and Sharon Lechter, my partner and co-author, I doubt if I would have become a *New York Times* and *Wall Street Journal* best-selling author today.

Most importantly, I took my dad's advice and made the best of a bad situation. Looking back, I can see how failing English and almost the tenth grade was a blessing in disguise. The incident caused me to buckle down and make a few corrections in my attitude and study habits. I realize that if I had not made those corrections in the tenth grade, I would surely have flunked out in college.

## Rich Dad's Comments

His son's F in English from the same teacher disturbed rich dad. He was grateful that my dad intervened and set up a summer school program for us to make up our failing grades. Yet, he used the experience to pass along a different lesson to Mike and me.

"Our lives are ruined," I said. "What is the use?" added Mike. "We will never get ahead because of that one teacher. On top of that, we have to spend our summer in a classroom." Mike and I complained a lot after we failed English. In some ways we felt our future, at least our summer, had been taken away from us. We could see the so-called smart kids moving on and we felt we were left behind. Many of our fellow classmates walked by us and snickered. A few called us "losers." Occasionally we heard behind our backs, "If you don't have good grades, you won't get into a good college." Or, "If you think high school English is hard, just wait till you get to college." We tried to handle the rude comments that are common among kids, and we tried to laugh it off. Yet, deep down, it still hurt. The truth was that we did feel like failures and we did feel that we were being left behind.

One day after summer school, Mike and I were sitting in rich dad's office, discussing our classmates' comments and how we felt about them. Rich dad overheard us, sat down, looked the two of us straight in the eye, and said, "I'm tired of you two boys whining and complaining. I'm tired of the two of you thinking like victims and acting like losers." He sat there glaring at us. "Enough is enough. You failed. So what? Just because you failed once doesn't make you a failure. Just look at how many times I've failed. So stop feeling sorry for yourselves and stop letting your classmates get to you."

"But we now have bad grades," I protested. "Those bad grades will stay with us forever. How will we get into a good college or university?"

"Look," said rich dad. "If you two boys let one bad grade ruin your life, you have no future anyway. If you let one bad grade be your downfall, then real life would have beaten you anyway. Real life is much tougher than high school English. And if you blame your English teacher and you think that English teacher was tough, then you have a rude awakening waiting for you when you enter the real world. The world outside of school is filled with people much harder, much tougher, and much more demanding than your English teacher. So, to repeat: If you let one bad grade and one English teacher ruin your future, then you had no future anyway."

"But what about the kids that are teasing us and laughing at us?" Mike complained.

"Oh come on," said rich dad with a chuckle soon breaking into a laugh. "Look at how many people criticize me! Robert, look at how many times your dad has been publicly criticized. Look at how many times both our names have been in the news. How many times I have been called a greedy businessman and your dad an unfair public servant? If you two let a bunch of kids with pimples on their faces get to you and defeat you, then you really will be failures.

"One difference between a successful person and an average person is how much criticism they can take. The average person cannot take much criticism and that is why they remain average all their lives. That is why they fail to be leaders. Average people live in fear of what someone else may say or think of them. So they live their lives going along and getting along with all the other average people . . . living in fear of criticism. Living in fear of what someone else might think of them or criticize them for. People are always critical of other people. Look, I criticize your dad and I know he criticizes me—yet we still respect each other.

"But if people are criticizing you, at least they've noticed you. Be worried if no one is criticizing you," rich dad concluded with a laugh. "You've given them something to talk about. You've given them something to break the boring monotony of their lives. If you can learn to handle criticism, you are learning something valuable for your life," rich dad said, still laughing. "Look, 33 percent of the people will love you no matter what you do. Thirty-three percent of the people will dislike you regardless of what you do, good or bad. And 33 percent of the people don't care either way. Your job in life is to ignore the 33 percent who will never like you and do your best to convince the 33 percent in the middle to join the 33 percent who love you. That's it. The only thing worse than being criticized is not being criticized." He laughed heartily at himself.

"So even grown-ups live in fear of other people and being criticized?" I asked, doing my best to get back to the lesson and away from rich dad's laughter. He thought it was funny but I didn't see the humor.

Rich dad nodded and grew more serious. "It's the number one fear of most humans. It's called the fear of ostracism—the fear of being different, of standing outside the herd. That is why public speaking is the number one fear . . . a fear greater than death for many people."

"So people just join the herd and hide in the herd because they are afraid of being criticized?" Mike asked.

"Yes, and that is one reason so few people ever achieve great wealth. Most people feel safer in the herd of the average, living in fear of being criticized or being different," said rich dad. "Most people find it easier to be average, to be normal, to hide, doing exactly what the herd does . . . just going along . . . just to get along."

"What you are saying is that this whole affair of flunking English class could be a very good thing for us in the long run?" Mike asked.

"If you want to make it a good thing," replied rich dad quietly. "Or you can make it a bad thing."

"But what about our grades? Those grades will go with us for the rest of our lives," I added with a slight whine.

Rich dad shook his head and then leaned over speaking sternly, "Look, Robert. I will share with you a big secret." Rich dad paused to make sure I was hearing his communication directly and without distortion. He then said, *"My banker has never asked me for my report card."*

His comment startled me and jolted me out of my chain of thinking—the chain of thought that was saying my life was ruined because of bad grades. "What are you saying?" I responded feebly, not fully understanding where he was going with this statement.

"You heard me," rich dad said, also rocking back in his chair. He knew I heard him. He was letting his statement settle in. He knew that it was shaking a core value of my family, a family of educators.

"Your banker has never asked you for your report card?" I repeated quietly. "Are you saying grades aren't important?"

"Did I say that?" asked rich dad. "Did I say grades *aren't* important?"

"No," I replied sheepishly. "You did not say that."

"So what did I say?"

I blurted out, now able to repeat the statement, "You said, 'My banker has never asked me for my report card.'" In my family, report cards and good grades were almost sacred.

"When I go to see my banker," rich dad began again, "he does not say, 'Show me your grades.' Does he?" Rich dad continued on without waiting for an answer. "Does my banker ask, 'Were you a straight-A student? Does he ask me to show him my report card? Does he say, 'Oh, you had good grades. Let me lend you a million dollars'? Does he say things like that?"

"I don't think so," said Mike. "At least he has never asked you for your report card when I was with you in his office. And I know he does not lend you money based on your grade point average."

"So what does he ask for?" asked rich dad.

"He asks you for your financial statement," Mike replied quietly. "He always asks for updated P&Ls—profit and loss statements—and balance sheets."

Rich dad continued. "Bankers always ask for a financial statement. Bankers ask everyone for a financial statement. Why do you think they ask everyone, rich or poor, educated or uneducated, for a financial statement before they will lend them any money?"

Mike and I shook our heads silently and slowly waiting for the answer. "I've never really thought about it," said Mike, finally. "Why don't you tell us?"

"Because your financial statement is your report card once you leave school," rich dad said in a strong, low voice. "The problem is, most people leave school and have no idea what a financial statement is."

"My financial statement is my report card once I leave school?" I asked incredulously.

Rich dad nodded his head. "It's one of your report cards—a very important report card. Other report cards are your annual health checkup, your weight, your blood pressure, and the emotional health of your marriage."

"So a person could have straight As on their report card in school and have Fs on their financial statement in life?" I asked. "Is that what you are saying?"

Rich dad agreed. "It happens all the time. Often, people who had good grades in school have poor to average financial grades in life."

## Good Grades Count in School—Financial Statements Count in Life

Receiving a failing grade at age fifteen turned out to be a very valuable experience for me because I realized I had developed a bad attitude toward my studies. It was a wake-up call to make corrections. I also realized early in life that while grades are important in school, my financial statements would be my report card once I left school.

Rich dad said to me, "In school, students are given report cards once a quarter. If a child is in trouble, the child at least has time to make the proper corrections if he or she wants to. In real life, many adults never receive a financial report card—until it's too late. Because many adults do not have a quarterly financial report card, many adults fail to make the financial corrections necessary to lead a financially secure life. They may have a high-paying job, a big home, a nice car, and they may be doing well at work, yet they are failing financially at home. They may be too old or out of time when they finally realize they have failed financially. That is the price of not having a financial report card at least once a quarter."

## Learn from Your Mistakes

Both my dads did not like the fact that their sons failed in school. Yet, both dads did not treat us as failures. Instead, they encouraged us to learn from our mistakes. As my schoolteacher dad said, "Fail is a verb . . . not a noun." Unfortunately, too many people think that when they fail, they become a noun and call themselves *failures*. If people can *learn* to *learn* from their mistakes, just as children learn to ride bicycles by falling off bicycles, whole new worlds will open up. If they go along with the herd of people who avoid making mistakes, or lie, or blame someone else, then they fail to take advantage of the primary way human beings were designed to learn . . . and that is through making mistakes and learning from those mistakes.

If I had not failed scholastically at age fifteen, I might never have graduated from college and I doubt if I would have learned that the report card for life after school would be my personal financial statement. That mistake at age fifteen was priceless in the long run. The reason so few people achieve great wealth is simply because they fail to make enough mistakes. Mistakes can be priceless if we are willing to learn from them.

People who have made a mistake but have not yet learned lessons are often people who continue to say, "It wasn't my fault." Those are the words of a person who is wasting one of life's greatest gifts, the gift of making a mistake. Our jails are filled with people who continue to say, "I'm innocent. It wasn't my fault." Our streets are filled with people who lead unfulfilled lives because they continue to repeat what they were taught at home and in our schools: "Play it safe. Don't make mistakes. Mistakes are bad. People who make too many mistakes are failures."

When I speak to a group of people, I often say, "I am in front of you today because I have made more mistakes than most of you and I have lost more money than most of you." In other words, the price of becoming rich is the willingness to make mistakes, to admit you made a mistake without blaming or justifying, and to learn. The people who often have the least success in life are those who are unwilling to make mistakes or have made mistakes and have not yet learned the lesson . . . so they get up each morning and continue to make the same mistakes.

## Chapter 3

# What Is the Price of Education?

"If you think education is expensive, you should try ignorance."

— Dr. Dolf de Roos

I am occasionally asked, "Are you saying that a person does not need to go to school?" My answer is an emphatic, "No, I am *not* saying that. Education is more important today than ever before. What I am saying is that the educational system is behind the times. It is an old Industrial Age system that is trying to cope with the Information Age . . . and unfortunately, it is not doing too good a job of coping."

According to economic historians, in 1989, when the Berlin Wall came down and the World Wide Web went up, the Industrial Age ended and the Information Age officially began. The following is a simple diagram of this change:

### 1989

| *Industrial Age* | *Information Age* |
|---|---|
| Job security | Financial security |
| Job for life | Free agents |
| One profession | Many professions |

| | |
|---|---|
| Defined benefit pension plans (employer responsible) | Defined contribution pension plans—401(k) (employee responsible) |
| Social Security certain | Social Security uncertain |
| Medicare certain | Medicare uncertain |
| Seniority an asset | Seniority a liability |
| Pay raises based upon tenure | Pay raises a liability since many employers are looking for younger workers with more current technical skills willing to work for less |

## Why Job Security Is Not a Problem

My mom and dad grew up during the Great Depression. That historical event seemed to have affected their mental and emotional outlook. That is why they often emphasized the importance of "Get good grades so you can get a safe, secure job."

If you look at the economy today, the problem is too many jobs. Ask any employer and they will tell you they are desperately looking for good employees.

Today, the issue is financial security, not job security. In large part, this is due to the shift of paying for retirement from the employer to the employee, the shift from Industrial Age pension plans, defined benefit plans, to Information Age plans, defined contribution plans. There are three major problems with today's defined contribution pension plans. One is that they are to be funded by the employee and many employees are not putting any money into their plans because they need the money to live on. Two is that the plans are indexed to the stock market, which means if the stock market is high, the pension plan is high. If the market should crash, as it has in the last couple of years, so will the employee's pension plan. And three is that a defined contribution pension plan can run out just when the retiree needs it most.

Let's say the retiree is eighty-five years old and their plan is depleted. The former employer has no obligation to the retiree. In contrast, with the defined benefit plan of the Industrial Age, the employer would have supported the employee until the employee passed on regardless of age.

My biggest concern is over government Social Security programs and Medicare programs. You know these programs are in trouble when the politicians are making campaign promises to "save" them. Of the two, it is the threat to the Medicare system in America that concerns me most. As we get older, our living costs may go down, but our medical expenses skyrocket. One catastrophic illness could cost more than the person's home. Today, a growing reason behind many personal bankruptcies is not financial mismanagement but catastrophic illnesses. A friend of a friend of mine was recently injured in an auto accident. He was the sole breadwinner in the home, he had inadequate medical insurance, and had to sell everything he owned. To make matters worse, his youngest daughter was diagnosed with leukemia, and the family is now seeking charitable donations and assistance from anyone who will help.

## What Is Lag Time?

These are just a few of the reasons why I say that we need more education in the Information Age, rather than the same old education we have been receiving. In the world of business, the two industries with the longest *lag times* are the education industry and the construction industry. Lag time means the difference in time between a new idea's conception and its acceptance by the industry. In the computer industry, the lag time is about a year. In the aerospace industry, the lag time is two years. That means it takes only two years for a new idea to be conceived and then adopted by the industry. In the education and construction industries, the lag time is approximately fifty years. For people hoping the educational system will catch up to the idea that the Industrial Age is over, I doubt they will realize this until the year 2040 . . . which is one reason why so many parents are pulling their kids out of school and choosing to home-school them.

Not only can industries be in lag, but individuals can also be in lag. In the Industrial Age, it was Einstein's $E = mc^2$ that was the formula of the era. During the Industrial Age, there were two superpowers in charge and people lived in fear of nuclear war between them. In the Information Age, the World Wide Web has left no one in charge. Moore's Law is now in charge. And Moore's Law states that information and technology are advancing quickly. Today's interpretation of Moore's Law is that information and technology are doubling every eighteen months, which means that each of us needs to double our information every eighteen months, or risk falling behind. That is why in the Information Age, *what you learn* is not as important as *how fast you learn.* Today it is risky to receive advice from anyone with old information . . . and in the Information Age, old can be only eighteen months. You don't want to be taking advice from someone who is lagging . . . in other words someone with old answers. Old answers may work on the millionaire trivia game shows but they will not work in the real world.

## So What Kind of Education Do We Need in the Information Age?

In many ways, both of my dads were great educators. As I have stated in earlier books, they taught what they thought was important, but they did not teach the same things. Below is a list I created that summarizes the education I received from both dads. Although there are many different types of education, for example physical education, music and art education, spiritual education, which are all important, the following are the fundamental educational studies that are required for minimal security in the Information Age.

1. *Scholastic Education*: The education that teaches you how to read, write, and do arithmetic.

2. *Professional Education*: The education that teaches you the skill to work for money, such as learning to be a doctor, lawyer, plumber, secretary, electrician, teacher.

3. *Financial Education*: The education that teaches you how to have money work hard for you.

Obviously, all three educational focuses are vital. If one is not able to read, write, or do mathematics, life in general is very hard. Unfortunately, many students are leaving school today not well skilled in these fundamentals. On May 7, 2000, the *Arizona Republic* ran an article that began with the headline, "L.A. Schools to Hold Back Thousands." Paraphrasing, the article made the following points:

• The nation's second largest school system backed down from plans to flunk huge numbers of students this year.

• Los Angeles Unified School District officials originally expected to hold back as many as one third of the system's 711,000 students, or 237,000, but the promotion guidelines were relaxed, out of concern that mass flunkings could cripple schools.

That is correct. They needed to flunk over a quarter of a million students because they could not attain basic reading, writing, and arithmetic standards. Officials passed the students because the flunkings would cripple the schools. I wonder what this will mean to a student who is crippled scholastically for life? This is an example of an industry in lag. Obviously, students have changed but the school system continues with its traditional ways of attempting to educate. Personally, I found school boring, irrelevant, and I was not motivated by the idea that I needed good grades for job security, as my parents had been motivated. Scholastic education is more important than ever before, but our educational system fails to keep pace with the times, so a student's scholastic education is sacrificed while we wait for the system to change.

My real dad was at one time the head of the teachers union in Hawaii. Because of him, I understand why the union is important to the teachers and I do empathize with many of the teachers' concerns. I also empathize with the students and am concerned about the long-term impact of them not receiving an adequate education at this period of time when education is more vital than ever.

When you look at professional education, again, its importance is striking. For example, a person with only a high school diploma may earn $10 per hour, right out of school. If that same person should go to electrician's school, their hourly rate could easily jump to $50 or more. When you multiply that $40 per hour difference by eight hours a day, five days a week, four weeks a month, twelve months a year, over forty years, the investment in professional education is one of the best returns on time and money anyone can make. When you understand that most medical doctors invest an extra ten to fifteen years beyond high school to become a doctor, it is no wonder they feel they deserve a little bit more in pay than the rest of us.

Regardless if you do well in school or not, and regardless if you go on to become a doctor or janitor, we all need some basic financial education. Why? Because regardless of what we do or who we become, we all handle money. I have often wondered why we do not teach much about money in school. I have often wondered why the system focuses so much on grades and report cards, when in the real world, my banker has never asked me to submit my report card.

I often asked a few educators this question and I have heard responses such as, "We do teach economics in school." Or, "Many of our students learn to invest in the stock market." Or, "We offer a junior business program for students who are interested in business." Again, I realize that the people in the system are teaching what they know and doing the best they can. Yet, if you ask most bankers, they will tell you that they are looking for more than a stock portfolio or the student's grades in economics.

As my friend Dolf de Roos says, "If you think education is expensive, you should try ignorance." And for most people, highly educated or not, it is *not* what they know that is costing them money, *it is what they do not know that is most expensive.* Let us take just one subject as an example of lack of education . . . and that subject is taxes. Most of us realize that taxes are our single largest expense. We are taxed when we earn, spend, save, invest, and die. Now, compare the difference in taxes an employee pays as compared to what a business owner pays. The dollar amount over forty years is staggering. One of the reasons so many people who go to school, get good grades, and get a good job struggle financially, is simply because most of their money goes to the government—the same government that educates us, or fails to educate us. And taxes are just one small subject in the world of financial education.

Now compute the cost of what happens to a person who cannot read a financial statement, much less know what a financial statement is. Or what happens to a person who does not know the difference between an asset or a liability; good debt and bad debt; debt versus equity; or the differences between passive income, earned income, or portfolio income. It is the lack of this basic financial education that undermines a person's basic financial intelligence. It is this lack of financial intelligence that causes many people to work hard professionally, often earning a lot of money, but fail to get ahead financially. They may have job security, but many never find financial security.

My rich dad often said, "Financial intelligence is not how much money you make, but how much money you keep, how hard that money works for you, and how many generations you pass that money on to." One of the main reasons that poor and middle-class kids start with a financial handicap in life is that their parents pass nothing on to them financially. It is hard to include in your will your job and your company pension plan. I know, because my parents left very little money for their kids to move forward on, while rich dad gave his children millions of dollars in financial head starts. It is estimated that when John Kennedy Jr. died, he passed on hundreds of millions of dollars to each of his sister, Caroline's, two children. Take a moment to think how your life might have been different if you had a hundred-million-dollar head start? What could you do with your life rather than get up and go to work?

## *The Basic Financial Education*

When people ask me, "What do I need to know financially?" I always reply, "Find out from your banker what is important to him or her and you will know what is important financially." And that is why one of the best mistakes I ever made was to have bad grades in high school. If I had not had those bad grades in high school, I might never have realized that my banker does not think my grades are important. My banker only asks me for my financial statement and, as I said, most students leave school not knowing what a financial statement is.

Most people simply fill out a financial statement the bank provides them, instead of submitting their own prepared financial statements. And that is why most people think that borrowing money means *begging* for money, rather than showing the banker why he or she should *lend* you money. Always remember that a banker's job is to lend you money, not turn you down. Bankers don't make money unless they lend you money. That is why when a banker turns you down, it is like a teacher saying to you, "You have failing grades." Instead of getting angry at the banker, it is really a good time to ask him or her what you are *not* doing correctly and what you can do to improve your financial statement . . . which is your real report card once you grow up and leave school.

## *What Is Important on Your Financial Statement?*

Different people look for different things on a financial statement. As I have said in my other books, a financial statement is like reading the story of a person's life. A financial statement also shows the reader how financially smart or financially unintelligent a person is with their money. The following are some of the things my rich dad taught me to look for on financial statements. The financial statement used is the financial statement from my board game

CASHFLOW 101, which I invented to teach financial literacy, as well as the basics of investing.

## The Three Types of Income

For those of you who have read my other books, you may recall that my rich dad taught me the importance of the three different types of income. They are *earned, passive,* and *portfolio* income. Today, when I look at a person's or company's financial statement, I can almost immediately tell if the person is going to be rich, poor, or middle-class, just by looking at the income column.

This is the financial statement from CASHFLOW 101.
It teaches people how financial statements work.

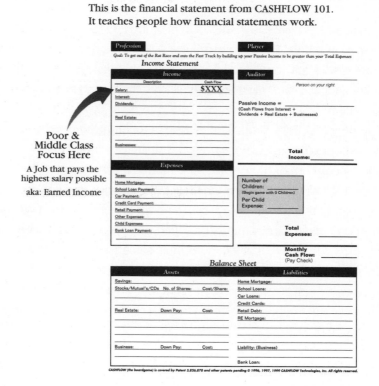

The above financial statement is of someone who manages their money like a poor or middle-class person. The reason is, the only kind of income is earned income, in this case their salary, which is by far the hardest income to get rich on. One reason it's close to impossible is that every time this person gets an *earned* income pay raise, so does the government. Another reason is, if you stop working, in most cases your *earned* income also stops.

The financial statement below is a financial statement of a person who has a good chance of becoming richer and richer. Why? Because this person already has passive income, which is income from real estate, the least taxed income there is, and portfolio income, which is income from paper assets such as stocks, bonds, mutual funds, interest-bearing accounts, and other such investments.

**A financial statement of someone who is performing the actions that make a person richer and richer.**

A Rich Person
focuses on these
types of income
aka: Passive & Portfolio

These are the incomes
that make the rich richer

The Kennedy kids never needed a job. They never needed a paycheck. Why? Because the earlier Kennedys knew that passive income and portfolio income are the incomes of the rich. The Kennedy children chose to work but it is obvious that they did not need to. If you had a hundred-million-dollar portfolio, the passive income and portfolio income would be more than enough to live the lifestyle of the rich and famous.

One of the reasons the CASHFLOW game is important for anyone serious about becoming a millionaire is because the game teaches people how to convert *earned* income into *passive* and *portfolio* income—the two incomes of the rich. It is virtually impossible to become rich *only* on earned income . . . and unfortunately, that is what most people are trying to do. One of the reasons so many lottery winners go broke is because they fail to convert earned income into either passive or portfolio income.

But more importantly, the game teaches the players how a financial statement works, which is something that cannot be learned by reading a book or by just playing the game a few times. Since repetition is the way we learn, playing the game repeatedly can assist the players in mastering the technicalities of a financial statement, which is your report card once you leave school. By repeatedly learning how a financial statement really works, the game also reinforces the importance of *passive* income and *portfolio* income, which is the income of the rich. It also teaches the importance of knowing the difference between good debt and bad debt. By repeatedly playing the game, you begin to break up the core conditioning most of us have learned at home and at school, the conditioning of working hard for money. The game trains your brain how to convert *earned income* into *passive income* and *portfolio income*.

## Complaints About CASHFLOW, the Game

Let me share with you the three common complaints about the game:

1. *It takes a long time to learn.* I recommend dedicating two four-hour sessions to learn the basics of the entire game. Three hours playing and one hour debriefing the lessons learned with the rest of the players. Players report that the one-hour debriefing session is the best part of playing the game. The players relate the game to their real-life financial challenges. After the two sessions, you are better able to try different financial strategies in order to win the game. The game is much like the game of chess, which means there is not a single formula for winning. Each time the game is played, it will offer you different financial challenges. By solving the different financial challenges each game presents, your financial intelligence increases.

2. *It takes too long to play.* The game does take a long time, especially when a person first begins to learn. But the length of playing time decreases if the player learns to solve the different challenges the game presents each time. The object of the game is to consistently see if you can complete the game in about an hour. In other words, the length of playing time decreases as your financial intelligence goes up.

3. *It costs too much.* In the U.S., the CASHFLOW 101 board game sells for $195 and comes with a video and three audiocassette tapes. These learning aids add to the total educational package. CASHFLOW 202, the advanced game, which requires the 101 board to be played, sells for $95, and CASH-FLOW FOR KIDS (age six and up) sells for $59.95. The prices are high because production is limited and because of the first two complaints. We made the price high because we wanted people to know that this is an educational product created only for people who were serious about their financial education. In a market study, when the game was less expensive, people perceived it as a game of entertainment. We were concerned that people who were not serious about learning would return the game asking for their money back. The price of the games may come down as more people realize that the games are for education and our limited production runs increase. The games are fun once you learn them but much like learning to ride a bicycle, the first stages of learning can be challenging. The electronic versions of CASHFLOW 101 and CASHFLOW FOR KIDS, released in 2003, are also available through our Web site, *www.richdad.com.* It has taken several years of research and development to create the electronic versions because it was important to us that the elements of cooperative learning and debriefing be included in any electronic versions of the game. Not only are you able to play against computer-generated opponents, with others at the same computer, but we are very excited that you may now also play CASHFLOW 101 with up to four other people from all over the world, online.

So for now, the CASHFLOW games are only for those serious about their financial education. As rich dad said, "There are only two things you can invest. They are time and money." Most people are not willing to invest either time or money in their financial education, and that is why according to the U.S. Department of Health, Education, and Welfare, only 1 out of 100 people will achieve great wealth by age sixty-five.

We hope that this 1 out of 100 will change as financial education becomes more available. While we continue to complain that schools do not teach basic financial literacy, we decided we should develop an electronic curriculum for teaching basic financial concepts as a way for us to give back and help get the curriculum into the schools. This curriculum, developed with teachers for teachers, is found at the Web site *www.richkidsmartkid.com* and has four mini-games teaching the difference between assets and liabilities, earned, passive, and portfolio income, good debt and bad debt, and the importance of charity. Teachers and schools around the world can apply through this Web site for a free copy of the electronic version of CASHFLOW FOR KIDS. If our children can learn basic financial concepts at an early age, they will be better prepared for the world they will face as adults and have a better chance for financial success.

## *Who Grades Your Test?*

As stated earlier, one of the important reasons for receiving a report card in school is because the report gives you an indicator on how well you are doing and what you need to correct. By *not* knowing that your financial statement is your report card once you leave school, many people *never* really know how well they are doing financially. Many people fail to maximize their income potential and wind up struggling financially most of their lives. My poor dad, although almost a straight-A student in school, did not really find out he had failed financially until he lost his job at age fifty. The sad part was, although he knew he was in financial trouble at age fifty, he did not know what to do. All he knew was that money was going out faster than it was coming in. That is the price of not knowing how to prepare and read a financial statement and how to self-correct after you experience a financial failure. By playing CASHFLOW in school, children will better understand the importance of their own financial statements, and how to create them when they leave school, their report cards for life.

Again, turning to the financial statement from the board game CASHFLOW on the following page, you notice the line that reads *Auditor.*

Many times, when I have supervised the game being played in a seminar, I notice that the players fail to fill out the line for the auditor. When I ask them why they left it blank, they often respond with, "Is it important?" Or, "I don't need to have anyone check my work." At that point, I become more stern, letting them know that the auditor, in this case another player in the game, *is one of the most important aspects of the game.* The game wants to reinforce good financial habits, and having your financial statements checked on a regular basis is a financial habit essential for anyone who wants to be a millionaire. In other words, your auditor in many ways is like your teacher in school, who goes over your work on a regular basis, letting you know how you are progressing, and helps you make corrections if necessary. In the electronic version of CASHFLOW 101 the computer serves as each player's auditor, and you will not be able to move forward unless you have adjusted your financial statement correctly after each move.

My wife and I go through this financial auditing process twice a month as a habit. Our accountant comes in, our financial statements and checkbooks come out, and the details of our financial life are reviewed in detail . . . as I said, twice a month. When we were struggling and short of cash, this process was a painful one. It was like looking at a report card filled with Fs and Ds. But as we learned from our mistakes, corrected, and improved our financial situation, the twice-monthly auditing sessions became fun. It must be like receiving a report card with straight As, an academic pleasure I never knew. When Kim and I first started out together, in 1985, we were looking at financial statements with very little on them. Debt from my past financial disasters was heavy on the liability column and we had nothing in the asset column. It was very unpleasant to look at our financial statements. It was like looking at an X-ray of a cancer patient, only for me, it was financial cancer.

Today my entries in the asset column are substantial. The number of entries in the income column of earned, passive, and portfolio income has increased, and so has the number of zeros behind each number in the income column. Our income from passive and portfolio income is much greater than the expenses in our expense column.

In 1985, we had to work to survive but today we work because we want to work. I doubt if we could have done so without the financial education my rich dad taught me. Without my rich dad's financial education, I would not have known about the importance of a financial statement. I would not have known the difference between earned, passive, and portfolio income. I would not have known the importance of corporations and how to protect my assets and how to minimize taxes. I would not have realized the importance of a twice-monthly audit and why being tested and graded twice a month was essential to becoming a millionaire. That twice-monthly audit is just part of the price. Due to my rich dad's financial education, I became a millionaire without cutting up my credit cards, winning the lottery, or going on a game show.

## *My Income Column Today*

Today, Kim and I have an income column that looks like this, in percentages:

| | |
|---|---|
| Earned income | 10% |
| Passive income | 70% |
| Portfolio income | 20% |

A few days ago, a newspaper reporter asked me, "How much money do you make? How much is your paycheck?"

I replied, "Not much. And I would rather not tell you how much my paycheck is. I'll just say that it is probably not as much as your paycheck."

He shook his head and smirked. "Then how can you write a book on money?" He went on to say that he hated writers who wrote about relationships but had no relationships, and writers who wrote about money who had no money. The interview was over and he left.

Now that you are much more financially educated, you may understand why I replied the way I did. First of all, my paycheck is very small. *That is because my paycheck is earned income and earned income is the highest taxed income.* Another reason why my paycheck is small is because the passive income is income from royalties as well as real estate. Portfolio income is from paper assets, which include dividends from corporations, income from real estate investments, and interest.

As you may notice, one of the biggest advantages a little financial education offers is a tremendous amount of control over the amount I pay in taxes, which are our single largest expense.

## Professional Income

Another point to notice is that my income today does not come from my professional education. After graduating from high school, I attended the U.S. Merchant Marine Academy, where I trained to be a ship's officer on tankers, freighters, and passenger ships. I also attended a U.S. Navy flight school at Pensacola, Florida, where I trained to be a professional pilot. Today, none of my income is derived from those two professions.

The other point is that a lot of my passive income comes from a subject I failed in school. At the age of fifteen, if you recall, I almost failed my sophomore year because I could not write well. Because of that failure, I improved and today I am better known as an author than as a pilot or a ship's officer. The difference is measured in the millions of dollars. In other words, I have made much more money from my failures than from my successes.

As I stated earlier in this chapter, in the Information Age, many of us will have more than one profession. That is why in the Information Age, the issue is *not what you learned* but *how fast you learn.* Remember Moore's Law, which is interpreted as information doubling every eighteen months. And keep in mind that the number of right answers you knew or how good your grades were in school do not measure your success later in life. Your success is measured by how many answers you *do not know,* how many times you fail, stand up, learn from your mistakes, make corrections without blaming, lying, or justifying, and then move on.

## Definition of a Loser

So if you want to find out what is important for your financial report card, simply go see your local banker. Fill out your personal financial statement and hope he or she rejects you. If they don't reject you, simply ask for more money. After they reject you, sit down and ask them what you can do to improve your financial report card. The education you receive could be priceless and life-changing. As I said, if you want to find out what is important in the real world, ask your banker. They look at people's report cards every day.

But the question is, "If bankers know so much, why aren't they rich? Why are they still working for the bank, minding someone else's business?" The answer is found in a subject I covered earlier in this book—Newton's law that states that, "For every action, there is an equal and opposite reaction." The answer is also found in the explanation of why in order to be a good, honest, and successful policeman, a policeman must also be a good crook. Or why every coin has two sides, a bird has two wings, and we have two legs, arms, eyes, and so forth. The reason most bankers are not rich is because they are too conservative. In order to be rich, especially if you start with nothing, you will need to be a good banker as well as a good gambler, and most good bankers are not good gamblers. As rich dad said, "You have to pay twice the price." And to be rich, you have to pay the price of being both a good banker and a good gambler, and most people are neither.

Rich dad said to Mike and me, "The reason most bankers are not rich is because most bankers are not gamblers. And the reason most gamblers are not rich is because most gamblers are not good bankers."

I then asked him, "Are most people one or the other? Either a gambler or a banker?"

To which he replied, "No. Unfortunately, most people are financial losers."

"Losers," I recoiled. "Isn't that a very harsh thing to say about people?"

"I said financial losers," rich dad replied in his defense. "I don't mean to insult anyone. Let me give you the definition of a loser before you think of me as unkind."

"Yes, please give me your definition," I replied, also a little defensively.

"My definition of a loser is someone who cannot afford to lose," said rich dad.

"Someone who cannot afford to lose?" I repeated the statement, doing my best to understand rich dad's definition.

"Let me explain further," said rich dad calmly. "When it comes to money, most adults cannot afford to lose. Many people today live on what I call the 'red line.' As you know from your interest in cars, the car's red line is that point where the engine's rpm's are so high that if you step on the gas any harder, the engine comes apart."

"So every dollar that is coming in as income is going out as an expense," Mike jumped in.

"That's correct," said rich dad. "So they cannot afford to lose because financially they have already lost." Rich dad paused for a bit to read our eyes and then said, "It's very sad. Millions of people all over this country, the richest country in the world, live at their financial red line."

"And," I concluded, "those are often the people who say, 'Investing is risky.' Or, 'What if I lose my money?' People often say such things or cling to their money extra tightly because they know they have already lost the financial battle."

Rich dad nodded. "You see, a true gambler realizes that winning and losing go hand in hand. Professional gamblers do not delude themselves that they can only win. True gamblers know that they too can lose. Gamblers know that they often lose in order to win."

"So that is why, if you want to be rich, you have to be a banker as well as a gambler," I added, beginning to understand more. The idea that a good cop also needs to be a good crook began to make more sense.

"And that is why people who have good grades do not necessarily do well in the real world," said Mike. "Real life is not made up of right answers. Real life is made up of multiple guesses, some of which turn out to be right and many of which wind up being wrong."

Rich dad nodded his head. "And that is why so many of the richest people in the world were often people who made the most mistakes. J. Paul Getty was known for drilling many dry holes in his quest for oil. He was famous for dry holes. But what made him rich was that he finally drilled one that hit one of the biggest oil fields in the world. The same is true for Thomas Edison, the man who reportedly failed 10,000 times before inventing the electric light. The reason I say most people are losers is simply because they live their lives unable to afford even one little failure. To be successful, you must be both a banker and a gambler so you *can afford to lose,* because every gambler knows that *losing* is part of *winning.*"

I created my board game CASHFLOW after rich dad's teachings. In the game, you will learn how to be a banker as well as a gambler. Too many people today want to put their money in safe, risk-free investments. I am afraid that many of these people will wind up the big losers in life. While they may never lose, they may also never really win. These are the people who plan on becoming rich by being frugal, safe, living below their means, and cutting up their credit cards. As rich dad said, "You can be rich by being cheap. The problem is, you're still cheap."

## How Much Can You Afford to Lose?

One of the reasons so many people play the lottery is because most people can afford to lose a dollar. The reason so many people play the dollar slot machines in the casinos is because they can afford to lose a few dollars. The problem is, for at least 60 percent of the American population, they cannot afford to lose much more than a few dollars. That's because they have already financially lost the game of life. Many people will not find out how badly they have lost until they lose their job or have to stop working due to age or medical disability. Hopefully, they will have family members who can afford to and are willing to take care of them. These are the people who live at their red line of life so deeply buried in bad debt. They are so concerned with survival that they cannot even imagine a life of wealth. We have a chapter called "Take Control of Your Cash Flow" in our book *Rich Dad's CASHFLOW Quadrant* to help these people start with a plan for shedding their bad debt. If followed, the formula will help someone get out of debt within five to seven years. The six simple steps have been reproduced on pages 59–60 in this book for your reference.

These same people also believe that getting rich is a function of luck. At one of my talks, a person asked me this question, "How much does luck play into your finances?" My reply was an answer given to me, but I'm afraid I do not remember the person who gave it to me. So I thank that individual and I apologize for not remembering your name . . . but I did remember your answer. And the answer is, "The acronym for luck means"

**L**aboring
**U**nder
**C**orrect
**K**nowledge

They other day, my wife and I lost $120,000 in a bad, very speculative investment. A close friend was very upset, almost as if it were *his* money. He said

to Kim and me, "The two of you are unlucky." Kim and I did not say much because there is no real reason to speak to someone who lives in fear of losing.
We did not tell him that we had also made about a million dollars and had lost
only $120,000 in our portfolio. We also did not tell him that we really felt lucky
because of two reasons. Reason number one is that we learned a lot more
from that $120,000 loss than from the million-dollar win. In other words, we
gain more knowledge from our mistakes. The second reason is because we
felt lucky that we could afford to lose that much money and not feel bad
about it. Back in 1985, we were in the group of people who could not afford
to lose anything.

## Chapter 4

# What Is the Price of Cutting Up Your Credit Cards?

"You must know the difference between good debt and bad debt."

— RICH DAD

So what is wrong with cutting up your credit cards?

To me, cutting up your credit cards is much the same as a person who needs to lose weight and who goes on a crash diet. Faithfully, one diets for a month, living only on three carrot sticks per meal, and for dessert after dinner you have four ounces of plain yogurt. After thirty days you cannot stand the pain any longer. One day in the mall, a young worker from the chocolate chip cookie company offers you one small sample. The aroma of those fresh-baked cookies is overpowering to the senses, so you say to yourself, "Oh go ahead. You've been good. Just have a small piece of that cookie." Suddenly, you find yourself buying a bag to "take home to the family," but the bag of cookies never leaves the shopping mall. The binge is on and soon you are ten pounds heavier than you were when you started the diet. The action of crash dieting leads to the reaction of overindulging.

The people that know me, know that I do not have the answer for the yo-yo diet. If I did have the diet that guaranteed permanent weight loss, I would be richer than Bill Gates. But unfortunately, I personally know only too well what it feels like to diet and then go back on an eating binge. In my family, I am the only one with a weight problem, a problem I have struggled with since childhood, so I cannot blame family genetics. While I do not have the solution for instant weight loss, I do have a solution for binge spending and credit card debt, and cutting up your credit card is not part of that solution. But again, my solution comes with a price and once more the question will be, "Are you willing to pay the price?"

## Beauty and the Beast

A friend of mine and his wife are models of physical beauty. They are slim, trim, and healthy. Dieting is not an issue for them. Working out at the gym is not a problem either. Managing their money is a different story. Both are in their late forties making a lot of money, but they also spend so much money, it frightens most people who know them. These are the people that pay off their old credit cards with their new credit cards. When they max out on their home equity loans, they buy a bigger house. In other words, they work hard making a lot of money, just to *push the string forward*. They also have a full-time maid and a nanny for their kids. They have more cars, more toys, more clothes, more lavish vacations than people making ten times more than they do. They are physically beautiful people but their beast is their lack of financial restraint.

   We have been great friends for years, so when we get together, they get on me for my lack of food and exercise discipline and I get on them for their lack of financial discipline. As I said earlier, we all have our different challenges in life. Mine is food and theirs is money.

## The Rich Have More Debt Than the Poor

I love spending money, but Kim and I are not foolish with our money. I love having the finer things in life. I love having the choice of flying first class or economy. I love tipping people well, if they have given great service. I also don't tip if the service was rotten. I love giving bonuses when extra money comes into the company. I love making my friends rich when our investments do well. I love the freedom that money buys. I love working if I want to and not working if I don't. So for me, money is fun, money buys me more choices, and most importantly, it has bought Kim and me the *freedom* from the drudgery of earning a living. That is why I do not understand people who say, "Money does not make you happy." I often wonder what they do for fun.

When someone says, "Cut up your credit cards," I don't think it makes people happy. One of the main reasons people spend money is to make themselves happy. Now, there are people who carry such need for financial happiness to extremes, just as there are people who exercise and diet to extremes. But in my opinion, the main reason cutting up credit cards does not work in the long run is because cutting back on doing things you enjoy does not make most people happy. Given the choice, people would rather have more money and have the freedom to enjoy life more. The only people who say "Money does not make you happy" are either people who already have a lot of money and are still unhappy, or people who would not know what being happy is anyway. In my opinion, it's not money that makes you unhappy. It's not being able to pay your bills or not having the money to do the things you would love to do, that tends to make people unhappy.

In the late 1970s, my company made millions of dollars very quickly in my nylon and Velcro surfer wallet business. Being in my late twenties, the money and success went straight to my head or, should I say, my ego. Each time I looked at the company's balance sheet and saw the money piling up, I felt more and more elated. I became cocky and arrogant. I thought that with each dollar increase, my IQ increased also. Unfortunately, it worked exactly the opposite for me. As my dollars were going up, my financial IQ was actually going down. Soon, I was into fast cars and faster women. The experience of fast cars and fast women was fun and I don't regret that time in my life, but it was a time that couldn't last. The pain of going from being a *paper* millionaire to suddenly being a person with nearly a million dollars of *real* debt, was a sobering experience. (Which is why I am concerned with so many people today who have their portfolios filled with *paper* assets, feeling rich. There is a very big difference between *paper* assets and *real* assets, *paper* wealth and *real* wealth.)

After losing my first million, I went to see rich dad to ask for his advice. Looking over my financial statement, all he could do was shake his head and finally say, "This is a financial train wreck." And then he proceeded to chew me out. Yet, as I said about the value of mistakes, that "financial train wreck" and the reprimand that followed were some of the best lessons of my life. The value from that mistake has been priceless and continues to serve me well today. Although that failure cost me nearly a million dollars, in the long term it also made me many more millions and will continue to make me even more money in the future. As stated earlier, making a mistake and learning from it can be a priceless experience. Making a mistake, then lying, blaming, denying, or pretending you did not make a mistake, is a waste of a good mistake. Today, when I find myself in the middle of a new mistake, I say to myself, "Keep your head. Don't blow your cool. Pay attention, and learn from this experience. This seemingly bad experience will serve you well if you are willing to learn from it. Pay attention and learn as much as you can while you're in the middle of it."

Becoming a paper millionaire in my late twenties and then becoming a loser with a million dollars in real debt was a horrible experience. I wish I could say I paid attention and truly appreciated the experience while the house of cards was coming down. But I didn't. I blamed, I lied, I denied, and I tried to run from my responsibilities. The good thing was, I had my rich dad, who pinned me down and made me stop blaming and start learning one of the biggest lessons of my life.

## Good Debt into Bad Debt

After my big learning experience, and once rich dad was through chewing me out, he said, "You have successfully converted a million dollars of *good* debt into a million dollars of *bad* debt. Not too many people make such big mistakes. You can learn from this experience or you can run from it. You choose." As I said, mistakes can be priceless experiences, but when in the middle of one, it is often difficult to realize the value of your stupidity. Nonetheless, that "financial train wreck," as my rich dad called it, was filled with valuable lessons. One of the most important lessons I learned was to face my mistakes, learn from them, and try not to repeat the mistake. That was the most important lesson in a chain of many important lessons because I chose to "face the music," as they say.

Another important lesson was on good debt and bad debt. I did not really understand the concept, at least not as clearly as I did at that moment. My rich dad had often cautioned me about good debt and bad debt. He would say, "Every time you owe someone money, you become an employee of their money." He would explain that to his son and me that good debt was debt that someone else paid for you, and bad debt was debt that you paid for with your own sweat and blood. That was why he loved rental real estate and he would add, "The bank gives you the loan, but your tenant pays for it." I had heard the concept and I understood it intellectually, but now I was learning the difference between good debt and bad debt with my body, my mind, and my spirit. Today when I see people simply rolling their credit card debt into a home equity loan I cringe. They may think it's a good idea, and the government offers you a tax break for doing so, but today I know better.

All they have done is take very expensive short-term bad debt and turned it into less expensive long-term bad debt. It may bring them temporary relief but it does not solve the problem. They have turned their credit card debt into a second mortgage, and for those of you who have read my other books, you know that the word *mortgage* comes from the Old French word *mort,* which means *death.* In other words, *mortir* means "an engagement until death." Like my friends who work hard only to get deeper in debt, they continue to push the string forward, and not learn the lesson. Unless something changes, they will be engaged until death with bad debt.

After I lost everything, I felt terrible, blamed others for my mistakes, and wanted to run from my problems. Rich dad forced me to face my mistakes. Going over the numbers was a painful yet very useful process. By facing my mistakes, it was obvious that I could not possibly work hard enough to pay off all the debt. Most people only lose a little at a time, pushing the string of debt slowly forward. But when you lose a lot of money, the pain and reality of a lot of bad debt is sobering. It was life-changing for me. When you lose $100,000, or are $100,000 in debt, it is possible for most people to physically work hard and pay off that much debt. But when it's a million dollars, hard physical work was not going to cut it, at least with my limited earning capacity.

Once rich dad had calmed down, he looked at me and said, "You can walk away from this experience and pretend it never happened. Or you can make it the best experience of your life." For those of you who have read our second book, *Rich Dad's CASHFLOW Quadrant,* and our third book, *Rich Dad's Guide to Investing,* you know about my work-out period and some of the different lessons I learned from the process.

On that day back in 1979, rich dad taught me one of the lessons that has proven priceless. On that day he said, "The rich have more debt than the poor. The difference is that they have good debt and the poor and middle class are loaded up with bad debt." Rich dad went on to say, "You should treat all debt, good or bad, the same way you treat a loaded gun . . . and that is with a lot of respect. People who do not respect the power of debt are often financially wounded by it . . . sometimes killed. People who respect and harness the power of debt may become rich beyond their wildest dreams. As you now know, debt has the power to make you very rich and it also has the power to make you very poor."

## Harnessing the Power of Debt

There are many reasons that I do not join the bandwagon that says, "Cut up your credit cards, get out of debt, and live below your means." I do not say it because I don't think that advice solves the problem for anyone who wants to be rich. For people who want to be rich, have a lot of money, and enjoy the lifestyle that money can bring, simply cutting up your credit cards and getting out of debt does not solve that problem . . . nor does it necessarily make people happy. I do agree that, on just basic financial principles, cutting up your credit cards is good advice for *most* people. But simply getting out of debt does not work for anyone who wants to become rich and enjoy life. If a person wants to become rich, a person needs to know how to get into *more* debt, learn how to *respect the power* of debt, and learn how to *harness the power* of debt. So if people are not willing to learn how to respect and to harness the power of debt, then cutting up their credit cards and living below their means is great advice. Either decision has a price tag attached.

## A Great Used Car

A friend of mine came to the house a few months ago to show me his new car. "I got an amazing deal," he said. "I paid only $3,500 for it, put in $500 for some parts, and it runs great. I could easily sell it for $6,000." He then said, "Come on. Sit in it. Take it for a spin." Not wanting to be rude, I did as he requested and took the car for a ride around the neighborhood. At the end of the test drive, I smiled and said, "It's a great car." But silently I said to myself, "It needs a paint job, the interior smells of old cigarettes, and I would not want to own such a depressing vehicle." Taking back the keys, he smiled and said, "I know it's not a thing of beauty, but I paid cash for this so I have no debt." As he drove off, white smoke poured from the exhaust.

## If You Want to Get Richer, Buy a New Car

My wife, Kim, drives a beautiful Mercedes convertible. I drive a Porsche convertible. Even when we were broke we drove Porsches and Mercedeses, or other fine cars. We did not pay cash; we borrowed money to buy them. Why? Let me explain with the following story, a story I often tell in my seminars. It is a story about good debt and bad debt, and enjoying the finer things of life.

In 1995, I received a phone call from my local Porsche dealer. He said, "The car of your dreams is here." I immediately drove down to his showroom to look at a 1989 Porsche Speedster. I already knew that there were only 8,000 of this model made over a three-year period. In 1989, Porsche devotees were buying them, putting them on blocks, and storing them. If you could find a collector who would sell one, the asking price was $100,000 to $120,000 in 1989. But in 1995, I was looking at the rarest of all the 1989 Porsche Speedsters. This was Speedster number one, the first ever built of this model, and it had the Porsche turbo body, which means little except to a dedicated Porsche fan. Since it was the first one built, it was the model that the factory toured all over the world at auto shows and was the car used for the photo on the brochure. The car also came with a special plaque from the Porsche factory. In 1989, after the tour was over, this car was also put up on blocks and stored in a warehouse. When a collector decided to sell it in 1995, the dealer called me. The dealer knew it was the car I had been looking for. The car may have been used, but it had only 2,400 miles on it.

My wife, Kim, watched me go into a hypnotic state as I walked up to the car of my dreams. I sat in the car, took hold of the steering wheel and inhaled deeply, smelling the rich scent of leather, which was still with the car. The car was absolutely flawless and the color was perfect, a shade Porsche calls "metallic linen." Kim looked at me and asked, "Do you want it?" I responded with a nod of my head and smile. "Then it's yours. All you have to do is go find an asset to pay for it." Again, I nodded, climbed out of the car, sniffed the tires, and smiled. It was the car of my dreams and it was mine. We put a deposit on the car, arranged financing with the dealer, and I went out to find the asset that would pay for the car. In other words,

I was going to find an *asset* to pay for my *liability* and use *good debt* to pay for the *bad debt*.

A little over a week later, I found a great piece of property, borrowed money to buy it, and the cash flow from the property paid for the debt on the Porsche. A few years later the Porsche would be paid off, and I would still have the cash flow from the property. In other words, instead of getting poorer from having an expensive liability, I got richer *and* have the car of my dreams, which is still mine today. We did the same thing when my wife found the Mercedes of her dreams.

## The Best Things in Life Are Free

There is a saying that goes, "The best things in life are free." And I agree. A simple smile can make so many people happy, and a smile costs nothing to give. A pat on the back with the single word, "Congratulations," costs nothing and it can brighten up a person's whole day. A sunrise or full moon costs nothing to appreciate. So in my opinion, the best things in life are free. What I am talking about in this section are the finer things in life that cost money. The kind of happiness I am talking about is the happiness one finds from material things. I am not writing about inner happiness, because material possessions cannot give you that if you do not have it. Inner happiness is free . . . and priceless if you have it. While each of us has free access to our own inner happiness, not all of us find it.

## The Importance of Standard of Living

If I were in high school, my friend's $3,500 dollar bargain-mobile would have been my dream car. I would have driven that car with pride and showed it off to all my friends. But when I was in my forties, driving around in a cheap car was not my idea of a dream. At issue is something called your standard of living, which is a measure of your material happiness and satisfaction. There are three reasons why being aware of your material happiness or changes in your standard of living is important. They are:

1. *Your standards change.* As we age, our standards change because we are changing. If a person finds their tastes improving but their ability to afford their refinements in taste do not change, that person may begin bor-

rowing, increasing their share of bad debt, in order to afford these changes. If your standards change, especially to the more expensive side, it is important to find ways of increasing your income in order to afford these changes.

2. *It is important to respect these inner changes in material standards.* A person's inner happiness can be affected if their material standards change but the person is not able to keep up financially with these changes. For example, I might be a happy high school boy with a $3,500 used car, but I would be an unhappy adult driving the same car I dreamed of in high school. Today, I meet many people who lack inner peace because they have not kept up with the changes in their desire for the finer things in life. I meet many people who are unhappy, living below their means, trying to be happy by only buying things that are cheap, affordable, but below their personal standards, which have improved.

3. *You spend less if you buy what you desire.* I am very happy with my car and my wife is happy with hers. We may have spent more being clear on satisfying our material standards, which includes our house and clothing, but we actually spend less in the long run in time, money, and happiness because we buy what we want.

## *The Lessons Learned*

Years ago, my rich dad said, "Some people believe that God wants us to live frugally and to avoid the temptations of the finer things in life. There are other people who believe that God created these wonderful creations for us to enjoy. It is up to you to choose what kind of God you want to believe in."

I tell this story not to tell you that I have the car of my dreams but because I want you to have the wonderful material things this world has to offer—without sacrificing your financial well-being and winding up in financial hell. I tell this simple story of my Porsche for the following lessons about abundance:

### Lesson #1: The Importance of Good Debt and Bad Debt

As stated earlier, rich dad stressed the importance of financial literacy and that your financial statement is your report card once you leave school. The following is a diagram of the Porsche transaction:

This an example of a financial statement
showing my Assets buying my Liabilities
aka: why the rich get richer

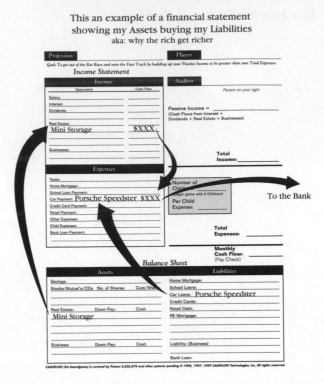

As you can see from the diagram of the financial statement, I borrowed money for both the real estate investment, in this case a mini-storage project in Texas, and for the Porsche. The cash flow from the investment covered the monthly costs of the Porsche. Because of good management, the cash flow from the mini-storage greatly increased and the Porsche was paid off two years early. Today, Kim and I have the real estate, the cash flow, and the Porsche. We did a similar process buying her Mercedes. So we got richer while we were also able to drive the cars of our dreams. Our friends, the couple who live above their means and who drive the cars of their dreams, get poorer instead of richer because the income from their jobs is their only source of income. They look good physically on the outside, but I suspect financial worries from bad debt are eating them alive on the inside. They are buying liabilities with bad debt, instead of assets with good debt.

Buying assets with good debt that provide the cash flow for paying for the things you want in life is what rich dad taught me. The cash flow from your assets represents your money working for you, something my friends and many people today still do not understand.

## *Who Are You Really Working For?*

When it comes to good debt versus bad debt, let me repeat what rich dad often said to me: "Every time you owe someone money, you become an employee of their money. That is, if you take out a thirty-year loan, you've instantly become a thirty-year employee. Unfortunately, they do not give you a gold watch when the debt is retired."

Rich dad did borrow money, but he did his best to not become the person who actually paid for the loans. That's the key. His advice bears repeating. He would explain to his son, Mike, and me that good debt was debt that someone else paid off for you, and bad debt was debt that you paid for with your own sweat and blood. His love of rental properties was based on "the bank gives you the loan—but your tenant pays it off for you."

Let me use a typical real-life example to illustrate just how this works. Assume that you find a nice little house for sale in a decent neighborhood. True, the home needs some fixing-up—perhaps a new roof, new gutters, and maybe a new paint job. But by and large, it's surrounded by other homes that are fairly well maintained, the neighboring area is solid, and the schools are good. Even better, the neighborhood is right next to a local state university, which is always looking for more housing for its students as the enrollment on the campus continues to increase year after year.

The homeowner wants to retire and move to someplace warm and sunny. He's asking $110,000 for his house. You negotiate a bit with him, and you finally settle on a price of $100,000. You already have $10,000 saved up in your bank account, so you need to get a mortgage for at least $90,000. But in truth, since that $10,000 is pretty much all the cash you have on hand, you decide to apply for a mortgage for $100,000. Why? Because with that extra $10,000, you can pay off the bank's closing costs as well as pay a local handyman to paint the house and repair the roof and gutters.

In most cases, the bank will be happy to give you the mortgage. Why? Because the mortgage is secured by the collateral value of the house. That is, if you went to a bank and asked for a loan of $100,000 and you didn't have any collateral or secured assets to back it up, the bank would tell you to take a hike. But with the house property backing you up, then the bank will gladly help you finance the loan. Remember, the bank is in the business of making loans—and will do so when they know that there's real collateral to help secure that loan.

Let's move on. Under current finance rates, the bank gives you a thirty-year mortgage at a rate of 6 percent. First, of course, they want that $10,000 as a cash down payment, which you give them. Once you figure in your property taxes, your monthly mortgage payment is going to be about $700. But as mentioned before, you don't want to be an employee of that bank loan for the next thirty years. The better approach is to have someone else pay off that debt for you.

Rich dad would suggest that once you close the deal and own the home, you then start talking to the local university about the availability of your home to be rented by students. Let's say that you charge $1,000 a month for the rent. If the home has four bedrooms, it could easily accommodate four students, each of whom would pay $250 a month. That's a fairly modest amount even for the most cost-conscious student.

Or, you can simply check with a local real estate agency to see if they can handle the rental of your property. For a small monthly maintenance fee, many real estate agencies will not only find a renter for your property, but will also take care of any minor handyman issues, such as fixing a clogged toilet.

Here's more good news. If your rental property is earning you $1,000 a month, and your mortgage payment is only $700, then your monthly net is $300 a month. This net income is what is known as *passive income.* That is, you're not doing any heavy lifting or hard labor to earn it. Someone else, your tenant, is paying off your thirty-year mortgage for you, and even better, you're earning an extra $300 a month.

Rich dad's real estate investing philosophy is primarily based on cash flow. Are you having a positive cash flow at the end of each month? But there is also the popular philosophy that real estate generally goes up in value. While you're earning that extra income each month, you're also paying down that mortgage month by month. That means that very slowly but steadily you are building more equity in the home. Since most real estate properties are believed to gain in value over time, your original investment of $110,000 in that home should also be appreciating in value. In other words, if ten years from now you decide you want to sell the home, the market value of the house might have gone up to $125,000. So, on paper, you would make a nice tidy profit of $15,000 from the sale of the house as well, as well as all the passive income you collected as well. But a word of rich dad caution: "Always keep your eye on your cash flow. Look at potential appreciation in real estate as a bonus, not as a reason to buy."

## Take a Tip from Those Who Have Taken Control

Take a look at one of my previous books, *Rich Dad's Success Stories*. That's a collection of success stories of everyday people from all over the United States (as well as a few from around the world) who were fed up living paycheck to paycheck. They just got tired and frustrated of trying to count the years until they could retire and then theoretically live off their 401(k)s (assuming that their 401(k)s still had enough money in them to allow them to retire). In that book, you'll find easy-to-follow firsthand accounts of people—some as young as teenagers, some nearing retirement—who have followed rich dad's advice and started to develop steady streams of passive income.

Many of those success stories are built upon real estate investing. All of the people in the book tell about how they had to overcome their fear of taking that initial financial leap of faith to find that first investment property and then making it happen. But invariably, once they started to see the stream of passive income develop, they almost all went back and repeated the process again . . . and in many cases, again and again. Some of those folks have gone on from simple one-family properties to larger properties, and all of them point to rich dad's advice as having led the way for them.

In some of the success stories, the individuals decided to invest in small businesses in order to earn their financial freedom. One of the chapters profiles a woman who started to invest in laundromats. As soon as she and her husband found that it was a fairly safe and easy investment to make, they then invested in two more. Now, she and her husband are doing quite well financially, and they'll be the first to tell you that it was simply a matter of doing some financial homework and making their money work for them, rather than them working for their money.

The point is that most people can't seem to get ahead financially because of the monthly onslaught of bills to pay. It's only when they finally make up their minds to do something about their financial lifestyle that they find the self-determination to look at other ways of generating money. And as rich dad says, if you want to get out of the rat race, then you had better start learning about the different types of income: earned, portfolio, and passive. Whether it's investing in real estate, or business, or other kinds of investments, the sooner you discover that there are lots of easier and better ways to make money than just having a job, the better off you and your family are going to be.

### Lesson #2: The Power of Inspiration

Let's get back to the used car story. When I drove my friend's bargain used car, I felt depressed. Sitting in the car did not inspire me. I did not hear angels singing and the heavens opening up with blessings as I did when I sat in my Porsche. As my friend drove away, with smoke pouring out of the exhaust pipe, I felt nauseated. In contrast, when I open my garage door and look at my Porsche, I still hear the angels singing. I love that car and I love the inspiration it gave me to go out and invest in another property. In other words, that car gave me the inspiration to get richer. Sitting in my friend's car only inspired me to take a bath.

I believe our maker assists us humans in building beautiful things. When I see a beautiful painting, or a beautiful home, or a beautiful car, I feel inspired. I feel the generosity, the beauty, and abundance of God, and it inspires me to go out and invest more vigorously—but by investing harder, not by working harder.

I notice that people who treat themselves poorly are often *not* the most inspiring people to be around. I have some close friends who are so cheap that when I am in their house, I feel like I am in my friend's used car. I love my friends dearly and I do not impose my financial views on them. But they work hard at living below their means, while Kim and I work hard to continually expand our means, and that makes a big difference in the way we live our lives. As I said, we are all different and we make different choices in our lives. I am simply sharing with you how my wife and I use the luxuries of life to inspire us to become richer.

### Lesson #3: My Banker Loves to Lend Me Money for Both Assets and Liabilities

My contention in *Rich Dad Poor Dad* that your house is not an asset has created a lot of controversy. In fact, I get more angry mail about that than any other point in my books. I often say, "When your banker says your house is an asset, he or she is not lying to you. He or she is just not saying whose asset it really is. Your house is *his* asset." I also state, "I'm not saying, 'Don't buy a house.' All I am saying is, 'Do not call a liability an asset.'" Still, the mail comes in. If you are uncertain about why your house is not your asset, but the banker's asset, you may want to reread my other books.

There is a point I want to take further in this book. Your banker will lend you money regardless if you buy an *asset* or a *liability.* Your banker does not tell you which one to buy. So if you want to buy a new speedboat, and your financial statements show that you can afford the payments, the banker will be more than glad to lend you the money. If you want to buy a three-bedroom home that you'll use as a rental property that makes you money, and your financial statement is favorable, the banker again will generally lend you the money. Why? Because regardless if you borrow money for a liability or an asset, *to the banker, either one is an asset.* So people who first borrow money to buy assets usually end up with more money to buy liabilities. People who only buy liabilities often have no money left to buy assets. The point is, since your banker does not really care which you buy, assets or liabilities, because either one is an asset to the bank, then maybe *you* should care. In fact, the more you care, the happier the banker is because the banker's job is to lend you more money, not turn you down for your loan. Bankers do not make money unless you borrow money, so the richer you become, the happier your banker also becomes. I love my banker because my banker lends me money to buy assets as well as liabilities.

## Lesson #4: What Asset Does Your Banker Love the Most?

A radio host asked me, "What do you invest in?" I replied, "I began investing in real estate in my twenties, so the bulk of my investments are in real estate today. I also own businesses and some paper assets such as stocks, bonds, and mutual funds."

The interviewer then said, "I don't like real estate. I don't want to fix toilets and receive phone calls late at night from tenants. That is why I don't invest in real estate. Everything I have is in stocks or mutual funds." He then ended the interview, cut to a commercial break, and I was ushered out of the studio.

## An Expensive Idea

Later that evening, I reflected on that interview. I said to myself, "What an expensive decision that radio interviewer has made. He does not want to invest in real estate because he does not want to fix toilets or receive phone calls in the night. I wonder if he knows how much that single idea is costing him?"

In our third book, *Rich Dad's Guide to Investing*, I wrote about the three primary asset classes a person can invest in. They are:

1. Businesses
2. Real estate
3. Paper assets

As I sat there quietly that evening, I could hear rich dad saying to me, "Which one of these three asset classes does my banker love the most?" The answer is real estate. Of the three assets, it is very difficult to receive a loan to start a small business. You might get a small-business loan but those loans often require you to pledge your other assets as security.

It is also very difficult to get your banker to lend you money to buy paper assets. Your banker may use your paper assets as collateral, and then loan you the money personally. *Rarely will a banker lend you money for thirty years at 8 percent to buy paper assets, but your banker will loan it to you to buy real estate.*

Years ago, rich dad said to Mike and me, "If you want to be rich, you must give your banker what he wants. First of all, your banker wants to see your financial statements. Second, a banker wants to lend you money to buy real estate. Just know what your banker wants and you'll find it easier to become rich." That is one of the reasons I said that the radio host's prejudice against real estate was expensive. It is an expensive idea because he will have to use his own, after-tax dollars to buy stocks, bonds, and mutual funds without the leverage of his banker's money. He had to use the most expensive money of all, his own money that comes from his labor, after the government has taken its share in taxes.

Let's use a $10,000 example to illustrate this point.

If the radio host buys mutual funds, all he can buy is $10,000 worth. If the host were to buy real estate, it would be fairly easy to buy a $100,000 property with $10,000 and $90,000 borrowed from the bank. I am also assuming that the property has a positive cash flow, which means that the tenants' payments cover all expenses and the cost of the bank's mortgage as well as providing some income. Let's say the markets are good and each asset goes up 10 percent that year. The mutual funds will gain for that investor $1,000 and the real estate will gain for the investor $10,000, plus the income from cash flow, plus depreciation, plus no capital gains tax (in America, if a tax-deferred exchange is used at the time of sale). The mutual fund probably does not have any cash flow, is not entitled to depreciation benefits, and is taxed at capital gains tax rates if outside a pension plan.

This is not to say paper assets are bad. I have substantial holdings in stocks and mutual funds. The point illustrated here is the cost of the idea "I don't invest in real estate." To me, the biggest expense of all is personal freedom. For Kim and me, the best thing about real estate is the monthly *passive* cash flow income, taxed at a lower rate than *earned* income, which allows us to be financially free. In other words, real estate allows us to have good debt, and good debt is debt that makes us richer quicker. But in utilizing leverage, or the bank's money, to get richer quicker, there is a price to pay.

If you look at the returns on your capital, by using no leverage, your return on $10,000 is 10 percent. But by using the bank's money, your return is 100 percent on *your* money. That also means that the real estate market would need only go up by 1 percent to have the same return as the paper market going up by 10 percent. When you factor in the tax advantages, the real estate market can improve by less than 1 percent to have the same net return as a paper market improving by 10 percent. Those are some of the reasons why rich dad said, "Always give the banker what he wants." And why he also issued these words of caution: "Always treat any debt as you would a loaded gun." The reason is because leverage can swing both ways with equal force, meaning you can make a lot more money using the bank's money—and you can lose a lot more money using the bank's money. So the price to pay is an investment in your education and several years of experience. If you are not willing to pay that price, do not use other people's money. Use only your own money and play it safe.

## Paying the Price for Education

As I mentioned earlier, in the 1970s, I invested in that real estate investment class, which cost $385. That three-day course has been one of the best investments I have ever made. I started slowly with small investments and invested another five years gaining the experience I needed. I too do not want to fix toilets, nor do I want to receive phone calls in the night . . . and

I don't. But I do like what my investment in real estate brings me, and that is a lot of good debt and a lot of freedom.

At a recent real estate seminar in Dallas, Texas, where I was the guest speaker, a man of about sixty years of age approached me. He had heard me say, "My rich dad taught me to be a real estate investor by playing Monopoly, and we all know the formula for great wealth found in that game. And the formula is, buy four green houses and turn them into one red hotel."

This gentleman came up to me and said, "Should I turn my houses into red hotels?"

I smiled and asked, "How many houses do you have?"

He thought for a moment and said, "A little over 700."

"What?" was all I could say in response to him.

Sitting down to find out more, I learned that he was a rancher out in West Texas. For the last forty years, he would buy a few houses a year and rent them out. He went through the booms and busts of both the oil and cattle businesses of West Texas. When it was a bust economy, he would buy houses from people who were in financial trouble, and often rent them back to them. As his cash flow grew he just kept buying more houses, most under $65,000, and he never sold any. At the time of our meeting, I found out that he was averaging $200 a month per house in positive cash flow. I gasped and said, "You mean you have over $140,000 in monthly income? Over $1 million a year just from rental property?"

"Yup," he said. "That is why I came to ask you if you think I should start selling some of my green houses and start buying some of them red hotels. It takes a lot of time buying those little green houses. So I like your idea of buying bigger buildings. Then I don't have to buy as many."

I shook my head and laughed and said, "The next seminar we have, I want you to be the speaker and I'll be the student." I then gave him the name and number of my financial and tax advisors and told him to call them. I told him that he was far beyond me. As he thanked me for the phone numbers, my mind drifted back forty years to memories of my rich dad playing Monopoly with Mike and me. I was playing Monopoly with little green plastic houses, and the gentleman walking away from me was playing the game for real. I could hear rich dad saying to Mike and me, "My banker always wants to lend me money to buy more real estate. So I always give my banker what he wants."

## Chapter 5

# *How Much Debt Do You Really Have?*

Before you can start on your way to financial freedom, you first have to pinpoint exactly how much debt you really have. For many people, figuring out how deeply in debt they are, is like going to the dentist; you know it's good for you, but it's not always pleasant. For some people, they have already given up. They know they're in a big hole, but don't want to deal with it.

But if you're serious about building positive cash flow in your life, you have to start with the fundamentals of financial literacy. Here's a quick quiz to get yourself going. Put a 1 next to any of the questions to which you answer yes:

Do you routinely pay your bills late?

Have you even hidden a bill from your spouse?

Have you neglected repairing the car because of insufficient funds?

Have you bought something recently that you didn't need and couldn't afford?

Do you regularly spend more than your paycheck?

Have you been turned down for credit?

Do you buy lottery tickets in the hope of getting out from under?

Have you put off saving money for a rainy day?

Does your total debt (mortgage excluded) exceed your rainy day reserve?

Add up the numbers in the boxes. If your score is 0, that's great! You're already in control of your cash flow. If you scored in the 1–5 range, you may want to think about reducing your debt by following rich dad's program. If you scored in the 6–9 range, watch out—you may be headed toward financial disaster.

## Rich Dad's Emergency Cash Flow Program

If you really want to gain control of your cash flow, you're going to need three key ingredients: figuring out where you are financially; personal discipline; and a game plan that's going to take you where you want to go. Use the financial statement from our CASHFLOW 101 game, included in the Appendix, to fill out your own financial statement.

Is it difficult to change your habits? You bet it is. It depends on you, and how eager you are to take control of your financial life. Remember, you don't have to do any of these steps. But if you don't, you'll just remain where you are, in the current rat race of spending your paycheck on bills that never stop coming (Unless, of course, you win the lottery. It's always amazing to me to see how many people think that winning the lottery is really a solid plan of getting ahead financially.)

But let's get back to reality. While you don't have to cut up your credit cards, you do have to follow a debt reduction plan. The first two steps in doing this are: 1) *Pay yourself first.* Whenever you get a paycheck, the first bill you pay is to yourself. Not the car payment. Not the mortgage or rent money. Pay yourself a decent bit of money, and then immediately put that money into a separate investment savings account. And don't touch it until you're ready to invest it in some other way. 2) *Your next step is to cut back on what I call doodads.* Those are those extra things in life that we all crave but really don't need. It might be a fancy car, or going out to dinner at expensive restaurants, or really sharp clothes. Whatever your doodads are, just stop that habit of purchasing them impulsively. Admittedly, this is where your self-discipline and willpower come into play. But if you really want to get out of debt, you need to adopt the old-fashioned virtue of delayed gratification.

Now if you have read our other books, you may think we are changing our advice. While rich dad believes in expanding your means to be able to afford any lifestyle you want, there are times when you have to stop and take other measures to get started on the right track. Remember that saying, "What do you do when you find yourself in a hole? Stop digging." Earlier I referred to people who are at the red line of life. They are barely making it from paycheck to paycheck. The following advice and the "Take Control of Your Cash Flow" formula from *Rich Dad's CASHFLOW Quadrant*, reproduced below and included in the Appendix of this book, are designed to help you take those drastic steps that will help you "stop digging" and start a plan for a better financial future.

## *What's Next?*

Okay, you've decided to discipline yourself and take control of your cash flow. Here are the next steps:

• Follow the "Take Control of Your Cash Flow" formula from *Rich Dad's CASHFLOW Quadrant*.

## *Take Control of Your Cash Flow*

1. Review your financial statement that you just created.
2. Determine which quadrant of the CASHFLOW Quadrant you receive your income from today:
3. Determine which quadrant you want to receive the bulk of your income from in five years:
4. Begin your cashflow management plan:
   A) Pay yourself first. Put aside a set percentage from each paycheck or each payment you receive from other sources. Deposit that money into an investment savings account. Once your money goes into the account, NEVER take it out, until you are ready to invest it.

Congratulations! You have just started managing your cash flow.

   B) Focus on reducing your personal debt.

The following are some simple and ready-to-apply tips for reducing and eliminating your personal debt:

### *Tip #1: If you have credit cards with outstanding balances . . .*

1. Cut up all your credit cards, except for one or two.
2. Any new charges you add to the one or two cards you now have must be paid off every month. Do not incur any further long-term debt.

*Tip #2: Come up with $150 to $200 extra per month. Now that you are becoming more and more financially literate this should be relatively easy to do. If you cannot generate an additional $150 to $200 per month, then your chances for achieving financial freedom may only be a pipe dream.*

*Tip #3: Apply the additional $150 to $200 to your monthly payment of ONLY ONE of your credit cards. You will now pay the minimum PLUS the $150 to $200 on that one credit card.*

Pay only the minimum amount due on all other credit cards. Often people try to pay a little extra each month on all their cards, but those cards surprisingly never get paid off.

*Tip #4: Once the first card is paid off, then apply the total amount you were paying each month on that card to your next credit card. You are now paying the minimum amount due on the second card PLUS the total monthly payment you were paying on your first credit card.*

Continue this process with all your credit cards and other consumer credit such as store charges. With each debt you pay off, apply the full amount you were paying on that debt to the minimum payment of your next debt. As you pay off each debt, the monthly amount you are paying on the next debt will escalate.

*Tip #5: Once all your credit cards and other consumer debt is paid off, now continue the procedure with your car and house payments.*

If you follow this procedure you will be amazed at the shortened amount of time it takes for you to be completely debt free. Most people can be debt free within five to seven years.

*Tip #6: Now that you are completely debt free, take the monthly amount you were paying on your last debt and put that money toward investments. Build your asset column.*

That's how simple it is.

## Other Tips to Help You Get Control

- Start paying all your bills on time to avoid any late fees.
- Find a credit card with a lower interest rate and no annual or transfer fees. Then you may want to consider consolidating your other credit

card debts to that one card. This will allow you to pay less in interest and fees.

• Stop using automated teller machines (ATMs) that charge a fee. That's like paying to use your own money!

## *You May Need to Get a Grip on Your Spending Habits*

• Get in the habit of paying cash. Use a charge card only for emergencies.

• Learn how to stop buying on impulse. Use your willpower to say no!

• Shop at wholesale clubs and discount department stores.

• Respect your budget! If you've reached the $200 food limit, skip the potato chips and ice cream.

• Buy generic medicines or find a discount pharmacy.

• Start looking for a part-time job, business, or other way to earn a little extra income.

• Turn your thermostat down. Turn off a few lights to save on your electric bill.

• Learn how to winterize your home from top to bottom. Insulate pipes. Get rid of drafty windows. Eliminate those areas where you lose energy.

• Cut back on your home telephone as well as cell phone usage. This is an area where many people overlook how they can save money.

• Check on your insurance policies. See if you can find some comparable policies for the same cost. Raise your deductible to lower your monthly bills.

In short, start getting in the habit of watching how you spend a dollar here and a dollar there. Give yourself a week and just check on how much you can save by not buying the expensive shampoo, or not going out to dinner, or cutting back on your lengthy phone conversations. Let's say you save $30 or $40 a week. Over a month, that comes to more than $100. Over a year, you're saving $1,200 or more—and that's a nice chunk of change to put toward paying off your credit cards.

Your goal should be to get out of debt as quickly as possible so you can start looking to a better future and start thinking like the rich. Then you can start buying or building assets that will generate the passive income to pay for your phone bills, electric bills, insurance policies, and more. That is the rich dad philosophy of expanding your means to live the lifestyle you choose.

### Secured Versus Unsecured Debt

There are two types of debt. *Secured debt* is debt that has collateral backing it up. Typical examples would include a home mortgage or a car loan. *Unsecured debt* is debt without any collateral backing it up. That usually includes credit card bills, personal loans, and medical bills.

The very first debt to try and get rid of is the unsecured kind. In the Rich Dad system, unsecured debt is most definitely what we call bad debt, and the sooner you can eliminate it, the more in control of your finances you will be. That means paying down your credit cards as quickly as you can, along with any other outstanding debts you may have.

Let's look at credit cards for a moment. No question that they are a wonderful convenience. And there really is no reason to cut them up, so long as you fully understand how they can lead to real financial concerns. For example, many credit cards charge you an annual fee just to have the card. Then, on top of that yearly fee, they of course charge an annual percentage rate (APR) on any monies you owe them. Take a look at your credit cards. Most these days are charging around 10 percent on your purchases and balance, but some charge much more than—even as high as 20 percent or 25 percent. Needless to say, you'll spend a fortune trying to pay off credit card debt if you only pay the monthly minimum fee. Get in the habit now of paying off new purchases on your credit card each month.

Where you can find the best APR rates? Easy. Check out the following Web sites to find the best rates and how you can transfer your current credit card debt to a much better APR:

- Bankrate.com *(www.bankrate.com)*
- Quicken.com *(www.quicken.com)*
- CreditChoice *(www.creditchoice.com)*
- iVillage:Money Life *(www.ivillagemoneylife.com)*

### Okay, Let's Focus on Getting Rid of Bad Debt

Here's the precise method I suggest for regaining control of your monthly cash flow:

Take all of your credit cards out of your wallet or purse. Following the formula for "Take Control of Your Cash Flow," check the various outstanding balances on each one. Take the cards with the smallest amount of debt on them, and pay them in full first. Then, once you have paid off those cards, call up the credit card company and cancel them.

From there, do the same on the remaining cards. Keep whittling away at that outstanding debt until it's gone. Please understand that this is a process that, in most cases, cannot be accomplished in just one or two months. Depending on how much cash you have, this process of whittling down your credit card debt may take several months, or even years. But do it—because it's a wonderful financial feeling when you no longer are a slave to those monthly bills. Even better, you'll discover that you now have extra cash each month to pay off other debt (like the debt on your home).

Once you have your credit card melted down, take the extra money you have and start to pay off the mortgage on your home. Most homeowners have the option of prepaying their mortgage. Check your mortgage contract to see if you can do this, or just check with your mortgage holder. In most cases, it makes a lot of sense for homeowners to literally save thousands of dollars by prepaying their mortgage each month. Even just tacking on an extra $50 a month to your principal payment (be sure you note that the money is to be added to the principal on your mortgage payment), you'll take years and thousands of dollars off your home mortgage.

The best news is that those individuals who have the willpower to follow these simple measures will find themselves financially solid and free of major debt within a matter of a few years. It may sound impossible to you in your current financial situation, but trust me—these measures will work for you.

## Emergency Measures

What can you do if you're really losing the fight against all of your debt? Truly at your own red line of life? Chances are you should check into some free or low-cost counseling. Here are some top resources to contact:

• The National Foundation for Credit Counseling (1-800-388-2227, *www.nfcc.org*). This nonprofit service, funded in part by contributions from credit card companies, offers educational programs and confidential credit consultation. For those who are deep in debt, a counselor will draw up a relief plan and negotiate favorable payment terms with your creditors.

- Debtors Anonymous (1-781-453-2743 *www.debtorsanonymous.com*). Modeled on Alcoholics Anonymous, this support group follows a twelve-step program to help members overcome compulsive spending.

## Chapter 6

# *What Is the Price of Change?*

"The definition of insanity is to keep doing the same thing
and expecting things to change."

— Popular saying

When I talk on the subject of good debt and bad debt I often hear questions
like the following:

1. But what if the market crashes?
2. But what if I make a mistake?
3. But what if I cannot pay off the debt?
4. But what if I am not interested in real estate?
5. But how can I afford to buy real estate when the prices are so high
   where I live?
6. But isn't all debt risky?
7. Isn't it better to be debt free?

These are all legitimate questions based on real-world concerns and are
not to be taken lightly. I heard one well-known investor say, "Treat all investments as bad investments." But you may also notice what the noted investor
*did not* say, "Your concerns are valid so don't do anything." Yet for millions

of people, these fears paralyze them and cause them to do nothing. It is the fear of the unknown that often causes people not to change.

Look one more time at the statistics from the U.S. Department of Health, Education, and Welfare.

At age 65:

| | |
|---|---|
| 1 | was wealthy |
| 4 | were well off |
| 5 | were still working because they had to |
| 54 | were living on family or government support |
| 36 | were dead |

It seems apparent to me that one of the reasons why only 1 out of 100 achieved great wealth is because most people were not able to change when they needed to change. They kept on doing the same thing. I am sure many wanted to change but were paralyzed instead by fears and doubts such as, "But what if the market crashes?" Or, "But what if I make a mistake?" Or, "But what if I cannot pay off the debt?" In other words, many people cannot change because they become prisoners of their own doubts and fears. Their doubts and fears force them to keep doing the same old things, hoping things will change, which is the popular definition of insanity.

## Newton's Other Law

Rich dad often said, "For people who are afraid of making mistakes, it is often easier to do nothing or do the same thing." Our Sir Isaac Newton's other universal laws, the Law of Conservation of Energy, states, "A body at rest stays at rest. And a body in motion stays in motion." In other words, a person often finds it easier to remain doing the same thing because a body in motion just stays in motion doing the same thing. And a person finds it difficult to change because it is often difficult to get something new started, because a body at rest stays at rest. So the price of becoming a millionaire often means doing something different . . . starting from scratch, getting a new ball rolling, making a few mistakes, and eventually becoming smart at something new. It sounds simple and it is simple, but the reason most people do not do something simple that could make them a millionaire is found in this law of Newton's.

## *Change More Than Your Job*

In my second book, *Rich Dad's CASHFLOW Quadrant*, I wrote about the four different types of people found in the world of money and business. The diagram below is the CASHFLOW Quadrant:

The four letters stand for: employee, self-employed or small business owner, big business owner, and investor. The book goes into the core differences between each of the four people found in each quadrant, and what changes people need to make if they want to change quadrants. The reason I bring the Quadrant up at this time is because while many people want to change, many more become trapped in their one quadrant. For example, many people leave school, get a job, and remain in the employee quadrant until they retire, although they may long to burst out and do something different . . . something different such as invest, or start their own business.

Many people, when they make a change, often make changes but only inside one of the quadrants. For example, many people make changes only inside the employee quadrant, which is why they go from job to job looking for more pay or happiness. As explained in my other books, the reason so few people become wealthy from the employee quadrant is because the tax laws are the hardest on the employee quadrant.

If a person does move from one quadrant to another quadrant, the most popular change is the change from the E quadrant to the S quadrant. A person making this change is often heard saying, "I want to do my own thing." Or, "I want to be my own boss." This is also a difficult quadrant to become wealthy in because if the person stops working, the income stops coming in. Also the tax laws are also very tough on the self-employed.

The B and I quadrants are the easiest to achieve great wealth in, but they too pose challenges, different personal challenges.

If you would like further distinctions or information on the four different quadrants and how to make the necessary changes, you may want to read *Rich Dad's CASHFLOW Quadrant* . . . and always remember Newton's Law of Conservation of Energy. *So my advice is to keep your daytime job and give yourself at least five years to start something new in a new quadrant.*

### To Improve Your Chances at Becoming a Millionaire . . . Just Change Quadrants

The reason so many people play the lottery, or game shows, in the hopes of getting rich is because most people are from either the E or the S quadrant. Most people who do find great wealth are primarily from the B and I quadrants. One of the ways a person can better improve their chances of becoming a millionaire is by changing quadrants. There are no guarantees, but at least your chances improve greatly as a person who operates from the B or I quadrant. *It is estimated that less than 1 percent of the people who achieve great wealth come from the E quadrant and the percentage is the same for people in the S quadrant.* In other words, if you are serious about becoming a millionaire in as short a time as possible, you may need to make a change in quadrants. I know for me personally, my chances for achieving great wealth would have been slim to none in either the E or S quadrant. I knew my chances were best in the B and the I quadrants and that is where I made my millions.

When I ask people, "Who *really* wants to be a millionaire?" I also ask the same people if they are willing to change quadrants. Some are and most are not. Why? The answer is again found in the word "change." For many people, the change required to move from the quadrants on the left side, the E and S side, to the B and I side is too high a price . . . a price greater than many are willing to pay. For people unwilling to make that change, it is best to find other ways to become a millionaire. Such as try and get rich by being cheap and cutting up your credit cards; marry someone for their money; or get rich by being a crook. But for those who are willing to consider making the change, I offer the following diagram, not discussed in *Rich Dad's CASHFLOW Quadrant,* as a helpful guide to you who are brave of heart . . . because that is what it often takes, a very brave heart.

## *The Guide to Becoming Rich*

I developed the following diagram in order to explain why simple book knowledge or classroom knowledge is not enough for total financial success. While the diagram can be used to explain many different things, for the purpose of this book, I will use it as a guide to explain what changes a person may need to make in order to become a financially richer person. I call this model the "Learning Pyramid."

If you have read our third book, *Rich Dad's Guide to Investing*, you may recognize this structure as a tetrahedron, which means a structure with four sides and four points to it. Some people call it a pyramid, and one of my teachers, Dr. Buckminster Fuller, said the tetrahedron was one of the most stable structures in the universe . . . which will explain why the pyramids of Egypt have lasted so long. Regardless, this tetrahedron is useful in explaining what the price is in making the necessary changes to becoming rich—or making any change for that matter. It also explains why it is so hard for many people to make the necessary changes.

One of my favorite quotes from Albert Einstein goes, "Great spirits have often encountered violent opposition from mediocre minds." I use this statement not to condemn those that disagree with my ideas. I use it to remind myself that I have both a great spirit and a mediocre mind.

To explain how the Learning Pyramid works, I'll use the following example. Let's say a person reads a book, and the book says go out and buy real estate or go find some good debt. So mentally they get the idea, "Go invest in real estate, acquire some good debt, and get rich" which is *not* a tough thing to do, but most people fail to do so. They may think about it mentally, but fail to do anything physically. Why? The reason many people are not able to *physically* go out and buy real estate is because *emotionally* they have a problem. And the problem arises when their *emotional* thoughts overpower their *mental* thoughts. When *emotional* thoughts are provoked by new *mental* ideas, we begin to hear the statements listed earlier, statements such as:

1. But what if the market crashes?
2. But what if I make a mistake?

These are examples of the emotion of fear rising up to challenge the new mental idea, even a simple idea such as, "Go and buy some real estate, acquire some good debt, and get rich." If the *emotional* thought is stronger than the *mental* thought, then the *physical* result is often no action at all. A person may go into what is called "analysis paralysis" and spend hours physically doing nothing but arguing internally with their thoughts and their emotions. Or the person may do as the radio host did during my interview and that is invalidate the entire idea of investing in real estate. You may recall the radio interviewer saying to me, "I don't want to fix toilets and receive phone calls late at night from tenants."

This is another example of *emotional* thinking overpowering a new *mental* idea. The radio host never gave the new idea a chance, thus shutting him off from the possibility of achieving great wealth and financial freedom faster. On top of that, toward the end of the interview, he said, "I thought you were going to tell us how to become millionaires?" To which I replied, "I did. I told you the way that many people do become millionaires and financially free is by having lots of good debt, but all you could think of was toilets." Needless to say, I have not been invited back on his program.

## *The Power of Ideas*

The radio host was not the only person who blocked out ideas that could change his life financially and in other ways. I do it. We all do it. We all do things that make us successful and we all do things that keep us unsuccessful. The point of this chapter is, how do we change when we know we need to change? As stated earlier, the definition of insanity is to continue to do the same things and expect things to change.

My rich dad said, *"One of the main reasons most people do not achieve great wealth and financial freedom is simply because they are afraid of making mistakes."* He went on to say, "The reason so many smart and well-educated people do not achieve great wealth is because in school they were taught that mistakes are bad. In the real world, the person who makes the most mistakes and learns from them—without lying, cheating, denying, or blaming—wins." So when you look at the diagram of the Learning Pyramid, one big reason people do not become millionaires, even though they *mentally* want to, is because *emotionally* they have learned to fear making a mistake. Rich dad often said, "It is the fear of failing that causes most people to fail." The fear of failing is an *emotional* idea that needs to change because that *emotional* idea often has more power than the *mental* idea, which is why so few people become rich.

## *What Worked in School . . . May Not Work in Real Life*

When my rich dad said to me years ago, "My banker has never asked me for my report card," one of the most important lessons I learned was that what worked in school might not work in real life. When I meet people who are struggling financially, I often find they're doing so simply because they can't break free from old ideas from family, friends, and school. In other words, they follow ideas they may not even know they are following—ideas such as "don't make mistakes" or "get a safe, secure job" or "work hard, save money, and stay out of debt." These are good ideas for people who cherish security over financial freedom. But they are bad ideas if you are a person who wants to be a millionaire as quickly as possible. So the price of becoming a millionaire is for many people the price of examining their old ideas and finding out which ideas need to be changed. But remember, when one mental idea changes, it often requires changing emotionally, physically, and spiritually.

By introducing financial literacy at an early age in school, we hope to make the new ideas of "buy assets," "have your money work for you," and "financial freedom" more possible and attainable.

## What Worked in War May Not Work in Peace

For me, the fear of failing was not an issue, as it is for many people. As I stated earlier, failing at age fifteen in school because I could not write was one of the best things that happened to me. Today I make more money as a writer than most of the students who were A students in English. From that failure, I also learned that my real report card was my financial statement. So for me, I knew that failing was a good thing, if I would learn the lessons from the mistakes or failure. I realized I could gain a great advantage by being willing to make more mistakes than people who were academically smarter than me. The problem was, while I learned a lot by making mistakes, it was my lack of fear of failing that also limited how much I could learn.

One of the reasons I volunteered to fight in Vietnam was because of the emotional and physical challenges going to war offered. While most people were saying, "I don't want to go to war," or, "I'm against the war," I decided it was best to go. So I volunteered in spite of the fact that I was draft-exempt. The good news was, the Marine Corps did an excellent job of training young men and women to overcome their *emotional* and *physical* doubts and limitations. We were trained rigorously to operate with cool mental thought even though we were emotionally terrified and physically challenged. We were trained to get the job done and fulfill the mission even at the cost of our own lives. That mental, emotional, physical, and spiritual training is what kept me alive in Vietnam. The bad news was, that training was also killing me when I came back from war. I have spent the last twenty-five years *unlearning* what I *learned* in preparation for war.

To survive in war, we are trained to fight in a split second. We often had to shoot before thinking, enter into terrible situations without regard for our own lives, and do horrible things even though we did not want to do them. In other words, we had to *physically* do things that we may not have wanted to do, and not let our *mental* thoughts and *emotional* feelings get in the way of doing our job.

When I returned from war, I discovered that my ability to overcome my fear and my willingness to fight were holding me back. In peacetime, there is no need for a warrior's behavior. I soon realized that there is a big difference between wartime Marine and peacetime Marine. People who become generals in the military are those who can be both good in peace as well as in war . . . generals such as Colin Powell and Norman Schwarzkopf. In peacetime, I needed to learn to think and act more like a politician or a diplomat even in the Marine Corps. I had to learn to be more patient, to think more before acting, to be kinder, less blunt, and less willing to fight at the drop of a hat. These are lessons I still struggle to learn today. I realize that I would be much more successful—financially, socially, and professionally—today, if I had made the changes faster . . . but I was not able to. As I said, I spent twenty-five years learning to fight and I had to spend another twenty-five years learning *how not to fight*.

The good news for me is that my ability to override my fear of failing made me a good entrepreneur and an investor. But those same abilities also became a limitation to my growth and success. As I wrote earlier, one of Newton's laws states, "For every action there is an equal and opposite reaction." For me, in my life, I needed to make serious personal changes if I wanted my success to grow. For me, my willingness to fight was causing me to win small battles, but I was losing the war. I soon realized that if I didn't make those changes, my success would be limited . . . just as limited as someone who was afraid of making mistakes. In order to grow, I needed to change.

As I said, every coin has two sides, every gambler also needs to be a banker. In my life, I had developed my warrior side for twenty-five years, and for the past twenty-five years I have been developing my diplomatic side. By having both sides, my success has grown. If I had only one side of the coin, I am certain my success would have been greatly limited. In other words, my strengths had become my weaknesses and in order to be whole and complete, I needed to make my weaknesses strengths.

## Life Is About Change

When people ask me, "What should I invest in?" or, "What would you advise me to do?" or, "Would you give me the right answer?" I hesitate and diplomatically back away from handing out *my answers*. The reason I do not like giving out answers is because right answers only work in school and on game shows. In real life, each of us comes with certain strengths, geniuses, and abilities. We also come with weaknesses . . . and as you may notice, our strengths are often our weaknesses.

To me, life is about change. To me, if you are not changing today, you may be in grave peril because the world is changing faster than ever before. The people who are in the most trouble are those who cling to old right answers and old report cards. With the Internet expanding its reach, the gap between the haves and have-nots will only increase. Today we have kids who are not yet out of high school who are making millions of dollars on the Web. They have not yet had a job and may never have to look for one.

As I have said in my other books, the idea of a job is an idea born out of the Industrial Age. Anyone clinging to old Industrial Age rules will financially fall behind those who adjust to the new rules of the Information Age . . . and believe me, the rules are different. If you are clinging to the idea of job security, automatic pay raises, and seniority, you are clinging to rules created in the Industrial Age. The good news is that there has never been more opportunity to gain tremendous wealth—but to gain that wealth, the price is that you may have to change.

## The Power of Your Spirit

The uncertainty of change is often frightening. I am as apprehensive of the unknown as anyone else. I have the same self-doubts as anyone else. I hate being wrong and making mistakes as much as anyone else. But the good news is that everyone has to change today. Due to the Internet, change is now democratic. Everyone has to change or pay the price of falling behind, slowly but surely. The good news is that we all have the power to get us through this change, if we want to access that power. That power is found on the Learning Pyramid, repeated below. And that power is the power of your spirit.

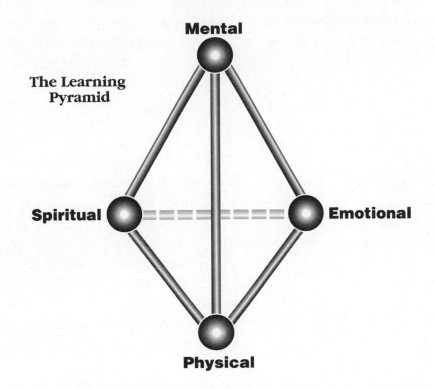

One of the best things about going to Vietnam was that I witnessed the power of spirit firsthand. If you talk to most veterans who saw actual combat, I am sure most will tell you of individuals who went far beyond the mental, physical, and emotional limitations that hinder most of us in day-to-day life. One of my classmates and dear friends from elementary school, Wayne, is a person who spent a year performing one of the most dangerous missions of the war as an LRRP. A LURP, as the acronym is often pronounced, and which stands for long-range reconnaissance patrol, was a person who was dropped behind enemy lines in a small fighting team to gather information. They often stayed behind enemy lines, living off the land for a week to two months.

One night recently, I was at Wayne's house in Hawaii discussing the changes we went through from growing up in Hawaii, going to college, and then going to war. We talked about how the experience of war dramatically changed who we are and what our core values are. We both quietly shared stories and spoke in awe of young men who performed feats of courage and heroism far beyond the so-called line of duty. The reason I tell this story about Wayne is because he made a point I want to make when I talk about the power of spirit we all have. During this late evening conversation, Wayne quietly said, "There were two missions where I was the only one to come back alive. I am alive today because dead men kept fighting."

I suspect that the reason so many Vietnam veterans have difficulties emotionally is because we fought in a war that we as a country did not intend to win . . . and those who came back are alive only because we had friends give their lives so that we could live. On top of that, we came back to a country that often spit on returning soldiers instead of thanking them for what they did, right or wrong. I too saw dead men who kept fighting . . . men who physically, mentally, and emotionally were technically dead . . . yet their spirits kept fighting on, so others could live. As tragic as such experiences are, the lessons learned about the power of the human spirit have been priceless in my and Wayne's lives. Today when I hear someone say, "But what if I lose some money," or, "What if I make a mistake?" or, "What if I fail?" I just sort of smile my diplomatic smile, nod my head, and walk away. It is still difficult for me to feel empathy for someone who is afraid of losing $10,000 when I saw others lose their lives.

We do not, however, have to go to war to find examples of the power of the human spirit, a spirit that we all possess. A few years ago, I went to a track meet for physically challenged people. There I saw another classmate who was injured in a car accident and had to have both of his legs amputated. Here he was fifty years old, both legs gone, and he was running the 100-yard dash on his new prostheses. As he ran, I did not see his physical limitations. All I could see and feel was his spirit driving him. As he ran, his spirit and the spirit of the others that were physically challenged filled the stand of spectators. Most of us began to cry as their spirits touched ours. I was reminded again of the power of the human spirit. I realized that although I was better off physically than he was, he was in far better physical condition than I was. His spirit had turned his physical handicap into a physical, mental, and emotional strength. We all have access to the power of that same spirit.

## We All Have Strengths and We All Have Weaknesses

As I have explained, I was not blessed academically. I am not what the school system would call a smart student. I was not blessed emotionally, simply because of my hot temper, lack of patience, and lack of attention to detail. I was also not blessed physically. I am not a great athlete nor was I blessed with great physical beauty. Yet, today I would say I have found personal happiness and financial freedom because I was always reminded of the power of the human spirit. Both my dads, as well as my mom, had that spirit and encouraged me to call on that power in times of great personal doubt. I am alive today because, as my classmate Wayne said, "Dead men kept fighting." I am who I am today because I married a woman who has a strong powerful spirit . . . a spirit that trusted me and stood beside me when others said she should leave.

If not for Kim's spiritual strength, I know I would not be where I am today. I would not be here today if not for my friends who stood by me and helped me up when I fell and lost faith in myself. I have attained financial freedom not because of my physical, emotional, or mental strength. I was encouraged by those around me to go on, even when I lost touch with my own spirit. I was able to make changes and grow to meet new challenges simply because other spirits inspired my spirit to carry on. And for me, I have always found freedom when I found my spirit.

There is a part of a poem I often say in times of deep personal doubt and darkness. I recently learned that its author was a writer named Ella Wheeler Wilcox, who lived at the turn of the century. The lines from the poem go:

> You will be what you will to be.
> Let failure find its false content,
> In that poor word environment.
> But spirit scorns it and is free.
> It masters time, it conquers space.
> It cows that boastful trickster chance,
> And bids the tyrant circumstance,
> Uncrown, and fill a servant's place.
> The human will . . . that force unseen.
> The offspring of a deathless soul,
> Can hew a way to any goal,

Though walls of granite intervene.
Be not impatient in delay,
But wait as one who understands,
When spirit rises and commands,
The gods are ready to obey.

It was because of my spirit that I was able to study and learn mentally, learn to harness my emotions properly, and take physical action—even though filled with doubt—to fall down, and stand back up.

# *What Is the Price of Fixing Your Financial Report Card?*

"Accounting leads to accountability."

— RICH DAD

I often hear, "I don't want to learn about accounting. I'm not interested in keeping an updated financial statement." When I hear comments such as these, I agree that it is a person's individual choice to learn what they choose to learn. At that point I often repeat a saying from rich dad, "Accounting leads to accountability." In other words, one of the benefits of studying accounting and continually striving to improve your financial statements is that the process improves your accountability to yourself. And being accountable to yourself is the price you need to pay if you really want to be a millionaire.

After I lost my first business, rich dad said to me, "When your car is broken, you take it to trained professional mechanics and they fix your car. The problem with your financial problems is that only one person can fix those problems and that person is you." Explaining further, he said, "Your financial situation is much like your golf game. You can read books, attend seminars, hire a coach and take lessons, but ultimately, only you can improve your golf game." One of the reasons so few people attain great wealth is because when people get into financial trouble, they do not know how to get out of trouble. No one has ever taught them the basics on how to diagnose the particular financial problem they may be in. As a result, many people know they are in financial trouble, but since they do not know how to read a financial statement, or how to keep accurate financial records, they do not know how serious their financial problems are, let alone how to diagnose the problems, or how to fix them.

Facing my ruined financial statement was a painful experience. Yet, facing the problems was the best thing I could have done. By facing my problems, rather than spending my time pretending I had no problems, I gained the best financial experience of my life. By facing my financial statement and facing my problems, I found out exactly what I did not know as well as what I needed to learn in order to fix my financial situation.

Watching me groan and moan as I faced the financial train wreck, rich dad said, "The good thing is, when you make mistakes, you make big ones." He also said, "If you are willing to face the truth and learn from your mistakes, you will learn far more about money than I could ever teach you." He went on to explain, saying, "When you face your own personal financial statement you face yourself and your own financial challenges. You begin to find out what you know and what you did not know. When you look at your financial statement, you become accountable to yourself. Just as a golfer cannot blame anyone else for their bad scorecard, once you look at your accounting records, you become personably accountable." As I said, facing my financial problems and solving them was the best education I could have received because by facing my mistakes, I became accountable for my own shortcomings. By facing my financial statement I found out that I had failing financial grades. I realized that I was not as financially smart as I thought I was. By improving those grades, I learned what I needed to learn in order to become a millionaire . . . and that is the price I paid. I paid the price because I really wanted to become a millionaire.

## A Final Thought

There are many ways to become a millionaire. One way is to cut up your credit cards and live cheaply. I chose not to do that because the price was too high. Another way is to marry someone for his or her money. And again, I could have done that, but the price was way too high, although it is a popular way to get rich quickly. Another way is to get rich by being a crook, but to me, that price is definitely too high. And another way to become a millionaire is to improve your financial literacy, your financial intelligence, and be willing to be accountable to yourself, your results, your continuing education, and your personal development in becoming a better human being. To me, that was a price I was willing to pay to become a millionaire.

Before finishing this book, I ask that you take one more look at a financial statement, as a reminder of what my rich dad pointed out as important.

**Summary of what's important**
aka: Financial Intelligence

Goal: To get out of the Rat Race and onto the Fast Track by building up your Passive Income to be greater than your Total Expenses

**Income Statement**

| Income | | |
|---|---|---|
| Description | | Cash Flow |
| Salary: | | |
| Interest: | | |
| Dividends: | | |
| Real Estate: | | |
| Businesses: | | |

**Auditor** — *Person on your right*

Passive Income = _____
(Cash Flows from Interest + Dividends + Real Estate + Businesses)

Total Income: _____

| Expenses | |
|---|---|
| Taxes: | |
| Home Mortgage: | |
| School Loan Payment: | |
| Car Payment: | |
| Credit Card Payment: | |
| Retail Payment: | |
| Other Expenses: | |
| Child Expenses: | |
| Bank Loan Payment: | |

Number of Children: _____
(Begin game with 0 Children)
Per Child Expense: _____

Total Expenses: _____

Monthly Cash Flow: _____  **Good Debt**
(Pay Check)

**Balance Sheet**

| Assets | | | | Liabilities | |
|---|---|---|---|---|---|
| Savings: | | | | Home Mortgage: | |
| Stocks/Mutual's/CDs | No. of Shares: | Cost/Share: | | School Loans: | |
| | | | | Car Loans: | |
| | | | | Credit Cards: | |
| Real Estate: | Down Pay: | Cost: | | Retail Debt: | |
| **Mini Storage** | | | | RE Mortgage: **Mini Storage** | |
| Business: | Down Pay: | Cost: | | Liability: (Business) | |
| | | | | Bank Loan: | |

Thank you for reading this book and I wish that you become a millionaire, if you are not one already.

# *Appendix*

**Profession** _____

**Player** _____

*Goal: To get out of the Rat Race and onto the Fast Track by building up your Passive Income to be greater than your Total Expenses*

## Income Statement

### Income

| Description | Cash Flow |
|---|---|
| Salary: | |
| Interest: | |
| Dividends: | |
| | |
| Real Estate: | |
| | |
| | |
| | |
| Businesses: | |

### Auditor

_____

*Person on your right*

Passive Income = _____
(Cash Flows from Interest +
Dividends + Real Estate + Businesses)

**Total Income:** _____

### Expenses

| | |
|---|---|
| Taxes: | |
| Home Mortgage: | |
| School Loan Payment: | |
| Car Payment: | |
| Credit Card Payment: | |
| Retail Payment: | |
| Other Expenses: | |
| Child Expenses: | |
| Bank Loan Payment: | |

Number of
Children: _____
(Begin game with 0 Children)
Per Child
Expense: _____

**Total Expenses:** _____

**Monthly Cash Flow:** _____
(Pay Check)

## Balance Sheet

### Assets

| | No. of Shares: | Cost/Share: |
|---|---|---|
| Savings: | | |
| Stocks/Mutual's/CDs | | |
| | | |

| | Down Pay: | Cost: |
|---|---|---|
| Real Estate: | | |
| | | |
| | | |
| | | |

| | Down Pay: | Cost: |
|---|---|---|
| Business: | | |

### Liabilities

| | |
|---|---|
| Home Mortgage: | |
| School Loans: | |
| Car Loans: | |
| Credit Cards: | |
| Retail Debt: | |
| RE Mortgage: | |
| | |
| | |
| Liability: (Business) | |
| | |
| Bank Loan: | |

# Robert Kiyosaki

Born and raised in Hawaii, Robert Kiyosaki is a fourth-generation Japanese-American. After graduating from college in New York, Robert joined the Marine Corps and served in Vietnam as an officer and helicopter gunship pilot. Following the war, Robert worked for the Xerox Corporation in sales. In 1977, he started a company that brought the first nylon Velcro 'surfer wallets' to market. And in 1985 he founded an international education company that taught business and investing to tens of thousands of students throughout the world.

In 1994, Robert sold his business and retired at the age of 47.

During his short-lived retirement, Robert, in collaboration with co-author Sharon Lechter, his CPA and business partner, wrote the book *Rich Dad Poor Dad*. Soon after he wrote *Rich Dad's CASHFLOW Quadrant, Rich Dad's Guide to Investing, Rich Kid Smart Kid, Retire Young Retire Rich, Rich Dad's Prophecy* – all of which earned spots on the bestseller lists of the *Wall Street Journal, Business Week, New York Times*, E-Trade.com, Amazon.com and others.

Prior to becoming a best-selling author, Robert created an educational board game – CASHFLOW 101 – to teach individuals the financial strategies that his Rich Dad spent years teaching him. It was those financial strategies that allowed Robert to retire at the age of 47.

In 2001, the first of the series of Rich Dad's Advisors books was launched. This team of professionals supports Robert's belief that "business and investing are team sports."

In Robert's words: "We go to school to learn to work hard for money. I write books and create products that teach people how to have money work hard for them. Then they can enjoy the luxuries of this great world we live in."

*Rich Dad's Organization is the collaborative effort of Robert and Kim Kiyosaki and Sharon Lechter, who, in 1996, embarked on a journey that would afford them the opportunity to impact the financial literacy of people everywhere and carry the Rich Dad mission to every corner of the world.*

# Sharon Lechter

CPA, co-author of the Rich Dad series of books and CEO of the Rich Dad Organization, Sharon Lechter had dedicated her professional efforts to the field of education. She graduated with honors from Florida State University with a degree in accounting, then joined the ranks of Coopers & Lybrand, a Big Eight accounting firm. Sharon held various management positions with computer, insurance, and publishing companies while maintaining her professional credentials as a CPA.

Sharon and husband, Michael Lechter, have been married for over twenty years and are parents to three children, Phillip, Shelly and William. As her children grew, she became actively involved in their education and served in leadership positions in their schools. She became
a vocal activist in the areas of mathematics, computers, reading, and writing education.

In 1989, she joined forces with the inventor of the first electronic "talking book" and helped him expand the electronic book industry to a multimillion dollar international market.

Today she remains a pioneer in developing new technologies to bring education into children's lives in ways that are innovative, challenging, and fun. As co-author of the Rich Dad books and CEO of that company, she focuses her efforts in the arena of financial education.

"Our current educational system has not been able to keep pace with the global and technological changes in the world today," Sharon states. "We must teach our young people the skills – both scholastic and financial – that they need to not only survive but to flourish in the world."

A committed philanthropist, Sharon "gives back" to the world communities as both a volunteer and a benefactor. She directs the Foundation for Financial Literacy and is a strong advocate of education and the need for improved financial literacy.

Sharon and Michael were honored by Childhelp USA, a national organization founded to eradicate child abuse in the United States, as recipients of the 2002 "Spirit of the Children" Award. And, in May of 2002, Sharon was named chairman of the board for the Phoenix chapter of Childhelp USA.

As an active member of Women's Presidents Organization, she enjoys networking with other professional women across the country.

Robert Kiyosaki, her business partner and friend, says "Sharon is one of the few natural entrepreneurs I have ever met. My respect for her continues to grow every day that we work together."

*Rich Dad's Organization is the collaborative effort of Robert and Kim Kiyosaki and Sharon Lechter, who, in 1996, embarked on a journey that would afford them the opportunity to impact the financial literacy of people everywhere and carry the Rich Dad mission to every corner of the world.*

**Robert Kiyosaki's Edumercial
An Educational Commercial**

## The Three Incomes

In the world of accounting, there are three different types of income: earned, passive and portfolio. When my real dad said to me, "Go to school, get good grades and find a safe secure job," he was recommending I work for earned income. When my rich dad said, "The rich don't work for money, they have their money work for them," he was talking about passive income and portfolio income. Passive income, in most cases, is derived from real estate investments. Portfolio income is income derived from paper assets, such as stocks, bonds, and mutual funds.

Rich dad used to say, "The key to becoming wealthy is the ability to convert earned income into passive income and/or portfolio income as quickly as possible." He would say, "The taxes are highest on earned income. The least taxed income is passive income. That is another reason why you want your money working hard for you. The government taxes the income you work hard for more than the income your money works hard for."

## The Key to Financial Freedom

The key to financial freedom and great wealth is a person's ability or skill to convert earned income into passive income and/or portfolio income. That is the skill that my rich dad spent a lot of time teaching Mike and me. Having that skill is the reason my wife Kim and I are financially free, never needing to work again. We continue to work because we choose to. Today we own a real estate investment company for passive income and participate in private placements and initial public offerings of stock for portfolio income.

Investing to become rich requires a different set of personal skills – skills essential for financial success as well as low-risk and high-investment returns. In other words, knowing how to create assets that buy other assets. The problem is that gaining the basic education and experience required is often time consuming, frightening, and expensive, especially when you make mistakes with your own money. That is why I created the patented education board games trademarked as CASHFLOW®.

## Rich Dad Poor Dad

What the rich teach their kids about money that the poor and middle class do not. Learn how to have your money work for you and why you don't need to earn a high income to be rich.

The book that "rocked" the financial world.

J.P. Morgan declares "Rich Dad Poor Dad a must-read for Millionaires."
The Wall Street Journal

"A starting point for anyone looking to gain control of their financial future."
USA Today

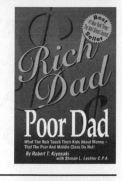

## Rich Dad's CASHFLOW Quadrant

Rich Dad's guide to financial freedom. Learn about the four CASHFLOW Quadrants and you will understand the most important keys to creating wealth.

The sequel to Rich Dad Poor Dad, Rich Dad's Cashflow Quadrant describes the four types of people who make up the world of business and the core value differences between them. It discusses the tools an individual needs to become a successful business owner and investor.

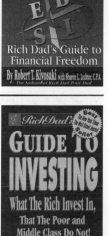

## Rich Dad's Guide to Investing

What the rich invest in that the poor and middle class do not. Learn how you can apply the techniques of the rich to create your own wealth and have it grow.

This is the third book in the Rich Dad Series. Rich Dad's Guide to Investing discusses what the rich invest In that the poor and middle class do not. Robert provides an insider's look into the world of investing, how the rich find the best investments, and how you can apply the techniques of the rich to create your own wealth.

## Rich Dad's Rich Kid Smart Kid

Give your child a financial headstart. Awaken your child's love of learning how to be financially free. Imagine the results you'll see when they start early!

This book is written for parents who value education, want to give their child a financial and academic headstart in life, and are willing to take an active role to make it happen. Rich Kid Smart Kid is designed to help you give your child the same inspiring and practical financial knowledge that Robert's rich dad gave him. Learn how to awaken your child's love of learning.

## CASHFLOW® 101

CASHFLOW 101 is an educational program that teaches accounting, finance, and investing at the same time...and makes learning fun.

Learn how to get out of the rat race and onto the fast track where your money works for you instead of you working hard for your money. The educational program, CASHFLOW 101, includes three audiocassettes which reveal distinctions on CASHFLOW 101 as well as valuable investment information and a video titled "The Secrets of the Rich."

CASHFLOW 101 is recommended for adults and children age 10 and older.

---

## CASHFLOW® 202

CASHFLOW 202 teaches you the advanced business and investing techniques used by technical investors by adding volatility to the game. It teaches the advanced investment techniques of "short-selling stock," "put-options," "call-options," "straddles" and real estate exchanges.

You must have CASHFLOW 101 in order to play CASHFLOW 202. This package contains new game sheets, new playing cards, and four audiocassettes.

---

## CASHFLOW for KIDS™

Give your children the financial headstart necessary to thrive in today's fast-paced and changing world. Schools teach children how to work for money. CASHFLOW for Kids teaches children how to have money work for them.

CASHFLOW for Kids is a complete educational package which includes the book and audiocassette titled "Rich Dad's Guide to Raising Your Child's Financial I.Q."

CASHFLOW for Kids is recommended for children ages 6 and older.

# Play CASHFLOW® with Rich Dad's INSIDERS!

## CASHFLOW® THE E-GAME

What's your dream? Freedom of time? Unlimited resources to travel the world? Whatever it may be, CASHFLOW THE E-GAME teaches you how to get out of the Rat Race and onto the FastTrack. Learn about money and finances in a fun, interactive environment to make more informed choices about money in your everyday life!

- Play and compete with others across the world in the online community through the multi-player feature.

- Discover how to become rich and financially free on a small or large salary!

How To Get Out of
The Rat Race

*To play the online multi-player feature of CASHFLOW THE E-GAME requires the purchase of the CD for $99 and subscription to Rich Dad's INSIDERS.

## CASHFLOW for Kids™ at Home

Discover CASHFLOW for Kids™, a fun game created to teach your child the subjects of money and investing. A families attitude about money is a powerful influence on a child from a very early age. The more your children play, the higher their financial IQ will become.

- Learn the difference between an asset and a liability!

- Discover the three types of income — Earned (where you work for money), Passive and Portfolio (where your money works for you)!

- Inspire an interest in the subject of money with your child!

## RICHKIDSMARTKID.COM  FREE!

RichKidSmartKid.com is an innovative and interactive Web site designed to convey key concepts about money and finance in ways that are fun and challenging...and educational for young people in grades K through 12.

## YOU CAN MAKE A DIFFERENCE

How?

Play CASHFLOW for Kids™ at School with family and friends and share the RichKidSmartKid.com Web site with your local teachers and school administrators. CASHFLOW for Kids™ at School is offered as a FREE download for your school from RichKidSmartKid.com.

**We'll do the rest!**

# What Others Are Saying About Rich Dad...

"Because of Rich Dad, I've learned that wealth is all around us. It's accessible and attainable. You can read books, you can seek advice...but playing the CASHFLOW game put things into perspective for me. It awakened the concept of becoming wealthy, of how rich people think, and what they do. This makes me want to continue my financial education to make a better life for my family."

– Roshiem A., Arizona

"Our children, Madeline (4 years old) and Makenzie (3 years old), absolutely love the interactive programs from Rich Dad. Madeline is already gaining real knowledge regarding investment and money matters through "Rich Kid, Smart Kid," which I find to be amazing at her age. It also provides a forum for me, as a parent, to begin discussing and teaching some of these concepts to my small children – something I probably would not do at this stage if it were not for your program."

– Jon F., Arizona

"I was a project manager/engineer and had worked my way up the corporate ladder for 20 years. I was finally making good money only to find that I was getting killed on taxes. On top of that, I could not picture myself working 9-to-5 for another 30 years."

"After reading Rich Dad's Guide to Investing, it dawned on me that I was directing an engineering team at work. So why not orchestrate my own real estate investment team? My team of advisors now consists of two lawyers, an accountant, two real estate brokers, an insurance agent, three mortgage brokers, a home inspector and – one of the strongest players on the team – my wife and partner, Connie. Life's too short to shortchange yourself."

– Larry N., Mass.

"The concepts taught by Robert Kiyosaki and the Rich Dad Team have had a major impact on our lives and our business. As tax and business consultants, the ways we serve our clients have changed and improved considerably. Everyone in our office now thinks in terms of "doodads" and cash flow and getting out of the Rat Race on a daily basis."

"One of the greatest impacts on our clients has been the CASHFLOW 101 game. For years, we have been looking for ways to instruct clients on accounting principals and tax strategies. CASHFLOW 101 is a terrific instructional tool for these concepts, as well as general investing and financial management. We play CASHFLOW 101 with clients and friends of the firm every month. These game nights give our clients the opportunity to broaden their perspective on money and investing, while allowing us to help them understand basic accounting principals, money management, and tax strategies."

"Thank you for creating a marvelous teaching tool in CASHFLOW 101 and helping us change the way we look at finances for ourselves and for our clients."

– Tom W. and Ann M., Arizona

# What Others Are Saying About Rich Dad...

"A friend of mine introduced me to the Rich Dad books a few years ago, and I introduced them to my Dad, a farmer who was just beginning to invest in real estate. My Dad and I then gave books and tapes to my sisters...and the family was hooked!"

"We recently closed on four townhouses (a "deal" my Dad found by being open to opportunities...) and know we never would have been thinking about cash flow and passive income if we hadn't read the Rich Dad books. We all financed our properties differently and our returns on investment vary – but we're all moving in the right direction."

"It is so exciting to constantly stretch and change the way we think about money."

– Sally D., California

"Thanks to Rich Dad I have the courage and confidence to tackle life's Big Deal cards – and create true financial freedom."

– Cindy O., Texas

"We were realtors focused only on earning our commissions.  And when we first heard of the book Rich Dad Poor Dad – from a "recommended reading" list given to us by our business coach – we realized that we were SELLING all the best deals...instead of capturing them for ourselves!"

"Thanks to Rich Dad we began to focus on the cash flow of our properties (instead of commissions) and ways in which we could leverage those properties to acquire more. Traveling the road to financial freedom has been an enlightening ride!"

– Curtis and Diana O., California

"A year ago I was drowning in bad debt and considering bankruptcy. I was frustrated and angry. My financial state of affairs — my financial ignorance — nearly cost me my family, my business, and my self respect."

"Rich Dad Poor Dad had such a powerful impact on me that I've bought a dozen copies and given them to my staff, my friends, and my college-age children. As a business owner, Rich Dad's Cashflow Quadrant helped me understand the BI Triangle and taught me to create and implement systems that strengthen my business."

"My Money IQ is rising everyday and I can say, honestly, that the Rich Dad messages have saved me from financial ruin."

– Dr. Randy R., Ohio

# What Others Are Saying About Rich Dad...

"My daughter, age 12, has been keenly interested in our pursuit of financial education as we read the Rich Dad series and play CASHFLOW 101. (She has played CASHFLOW with us and read Rich Kid Smart Kid.)"

"She often tells us of her future plans and one day we were outside gardening when she told me that when she owns investment properties she will also own a landscaping business so that she can care for the exteriors of her properties in a more cost efficient way! Her plan for the future now is to have her money work for her – through proper investing. We don't doubt it for a minute!"

– Kris P., Pennsylvania

"Three of my brothers – like me – are on fire with the Rich Dad materials! We have digested the messages and are moving full speed ahead with our lives with a deeply-renewed hope and passion! My brother (Joe) now calls himself 'Joe Freedom!'"

– Dan M.

"Robert Kiyosaki is blowing my mind away! I'm half way through the Cashflow Quadrant. I can't read enough! I have a whole new attitude – toward everything."

"I've been aware for a while that I knew damn little about money. I have been making myself read the business section of the Sunday paper for about a year and getting nowhere. I read Robert Kiyosaki's book in three days and I can see land! I love the direction and the hopeful feeling I am experiencing."

– Joe Freedom , (aka Joe M...brother of Dan M)

"I did everything my parents told me to do: get good grades, get a scholarship to pay for college, get a good job and be stable, stay at the same job..."

"My husband and I are now in our early forties, and more in debt and struggling financially than when we were in our twenties. Our eldest son is now a senior in high school, getting ready to go to college, and I don't want him to go down the same path that his parents did. My heart is heavy because I want the best for my family."

"I'm ready for another way, another path, another voice to guide me. My Rich Dad, Robert Kiyosaki, is that voice. I want to thank my Rich Dad for being there on that shelf, for lifting me out of the hopelessness I didn't realize I was living in, and for shining light on a better path for others, like me, to follow."

– Tia L., Hawaii

## What Others Are Saying About Rich Dad...

"A huge thanks to Robert for helping me shift my context. It has made a huge change in how I view the world. I have been reading your materials, listening to audios, and playing your CASHFLOW games for over a year now. It has helped me grow my financial literacy so much that my husband and I have begun investing in real estate. We just purchased our first property!"

– Valerie P., Canada

"The Rich Dad books have been a life-changing experience for me. Robert has given me the faith and courage to follow my convictions and prepare my plan for financial freedom. The Rich Dad books have given me the courage to take the steps to financial freedom."

"I have purchased two properties apart from my residence and while it's tempting to repay my mortgages, I intend to leverage the equity from these properties to invest in others."

– Kay G., United Kingdom

"Thanks to inspiration from Robert and Sharon, our lives will be different from 99% of the population."

"You have been our guiding light in our quest for financial freedom. Playing the CASHFLOW game has taught me more about business than business school did! You are making a huge difference in this world of financial illiteracy and chaos."

– Merced, Jon, and Jeff H., Utah

## What Students and Teachers Are Saying About CASHFLOW for Kids

"They can learn more in an hour of playing Cashflow for Kids than 10 hours of homework."

– Pam L. - Principal, Oklahoma

"I feel sorry for my mom, because (credit card debt) is hard to get out of and easy to get in."

– Carrie S. – 6th grader, Oklahoma

"One teacher asked the kids, 'If money was no object, what would you buy?' At the beginning of the day they wanted a car and by the end of the day they wanted a candy bar factory or other things to make money with."

– Michelle H., Scottsdale